WHAT PEOPLE ELEPHANT

This is an insightful and inforr
the tragic plight of captive elephants.
Bob Barker, television personality, activist, and philanthropist

Elephants Among Us: Two Performing Elephants in Twentieth Century America by M. Jaynes is a book everyone who cares about elephants should read. For someone like me who studies elephants living their marvelously complex lives in the wild, it is close to unbearable to know what the two captive elephants he writes about went through. But we have to know and this book raises our awareness and motivates us anew to prevent elephants from living miserable lives in captivity solely for our entertainment.
Cythia Moss, Director, Amboseli Trust for Elephants.

I grew up in India loving an elephant named Rani and know them as sensitive, loving, watchful, and cleverer than many humans. This is a deeply moving, true story of elephants who suffered at human hands: it is a book on a par with *Black Beauty* and *Old Yeller*. Highly recommended.
Ingrid Newkirk, President and Co-Founder, People for the Ethical Treatment of Animals

Jaynes tells the story of a captive elephant, and a sad story it is. These animals — intelligent, highly social, and used to large and complex ranges of habitats — simply do not belong in captivity. Like whales and dolphins, we can learn much from them, but we should only do so on their terms, not on ours.
Richard O'Barry, Director, Earth Island Institute Dolphin Project

I have looked into the eye of a wild elephant in East Africa and what I saw there I have never seen in the eye of a captive elephant. Gone is the pride of freedom, the solace of companionship and the sense of belonging. This book looks deeply into the eye of Stoney, an Indian elephant, and what Jaynes sees is a reflection of ourselves clouded with a collective shame upon humanity for the misery we create in our merciless search for profit from the exploitation of creatures far nobler than we.
Captain Paul Watson, Founder, Sea Shepherd Conservation Society

I grew up with elephants. They are among the gentlest, most loving, most intelligent of beings. Jaynes does us all a favour by waking us to the story of our relations.
Dr. Vandana Shiva, Ecofeminist, Activist, and Director of the Navdanya Research Foundation for Science, Technology, and Ecology.

To see ourselves reflected in all life is to finally and truly see. To cause harm and suffering to another being is ultimately to cause a tear in the fabric of ourselves. This book gives us a personal and powerful insight into the being and story of elephants and through that into the very depths of ourselves.
Julia Butterfly Hill, forest activist and author of *The legacy of Luna: the story of a tree, a woman, and the struggle to save the redwoods*

The story of Stoney and Mary must be told so that this insidious cruelty to such magnificent and intelligent beings can be understood by those who think it is acceptable to see elephants held in captivity. Whether the species is elephants or orcas in captivity, humans must cease patronizing the greed that destroys their freedom. This book is sure to awaken the masses.
Mark Berman, Associate Director, Earth Island Institute

The story of Stoney the elephant's long dark journey into night is unforgettably told. Jaynes deftly combines the experience of Stoney with that of his owners, the circus industry both past and present, U.S. Department of Agriculture officials charged with regulating circus animals, and the activists who tried to help this gentle, tortured soul. If any story has the power to wake people up to the plight of elephants trapped in the entertainment industry, and to the wonder of these great beings, this one will...this book combines description, drama, analysis, history, and emotion very movingly and informatively.
Karen Davis, PhD, President of United Poultry Concerns

Elephants are amazing beings. They have legendary memories, are incredibly smart, and deeply emotional. They experience the highest of highs and the lowest of lows. Sadly, these amazing giants have also suffered greatly at the hands of humans in a wide array of venues. If you ever doubted how amazing elephants are and wondered if they're as awesome as people claim, this book will change your mind, and especially your heart, Read it, allow the ups and downs to permeate your soul, and share widely.
Marc Bekoff, University of Colorado, author of *The emotional lives of animals, Animals matter, Wild justice: the moral lives of animals*, and *The animal manifesto: six reasons for expanding our compassion footprint*.

Jaynes writes with great care. This is an important book—Stoney was an individual, and his story as told in this very special book makes the case for affording all animals kindness and equal consideration. Whether you're an animal rights activist or simply a person who wants a world with less cruelty, you'll find that this book is for you.
Lisa Lange, Senior VP of Communications, People for the Ethical Treatment of Animals

M. Jaynes has rendered a moving narrative that restores at least some of what humanity has robbed from elephants around the world: dignity and voice. This book gives hope that we humans will soon re-discover the "elephant within us," and reciprocate the kindness and tolerance to other animals that they patently bestow upon us.

G.A. Bradshaw, author, *Elephants on the Edge: What Animals Teach Us about Humanity, and* Executive Director, The Kerulos Center.

Heart wrenching case studies make a compelling case for abolishing the use of elephants in entertainment. Read the book for details or just as a metaphor for the business-as-usual human domination of the natural environment that has brought devastating consequence to countless numbers of wildlife species.

Mike Hudak, public lands advocate and author of *Western Turf Wars*

Elephants Among Us

Two Performing Elephants
in Twentieth Century America

Elephants Among Us

Two Performing Elephants in Twentieth Century America

M. Jaynes

BOOKS

Winchester, UK
Washington, USA

First published by Earth Books, 2013
Earth Books is an imprint of John Hunt Publishing Ltd., Laurel House, Station Approach,
Alresford, Hants, SO24 9JH, UK
office1@jhpbooks.net
www.johnhuntpublishing.com
www.earth-books.net

For distributor details and how to order please visit the 'Ordering' section on our website.

Text copyright: M. Jaynes 2012

ISBN: 978 1 78099 706 3

All rights reserved. Except for brief quotations in critical articles or reviews, no part of this book may be reproduced in any manner without prior written permission from the publishers.

The rights of M. Jaynes as author have been asserted in accordance with the Copyright, Designs and Patents Act 1988.

A CIP catalogue record for this book is available from the British Library.

Design: Stuart Davies

Printed and bound by CPI Group (UK) Ltd, Croydon, CR0 4YY

We operate a distinctive and ethical publishing philosophy in all areas of our business, from our global network of authors to production and worldwide distribution.

CONTENTS

Acknowledgements   xii

Part I: Stoney, A Creature of Great Worth   1
1   Elephants and Humans   3
2   Birth and Early Years   5
3   The Easy Years: 1974–1986   7
4   The Lost Years: 1986–1994   17
5   Las Vegas   23
6   A Night to Remember   27
7   Isolation   33
8   Activism and Disgruntled Vets   43
9   The Death of Stoney   57
10   The Advocates   81
11   The Media Fallout   93
12   USDA-APHIS   103
13   Application   109

Part II: The Hanging of Big Mary   115
Epilogue: Further Adventures in Elephant Advocacy   141
And Finally   151
Afterword by Linda Faso   155
Appendix A   161
Appendix B   165
Appendix C   167
Notes   169
Bibliography   177
Images   194

For Erin

Acknowledgements

Let it be known from the very beginning that I am not an elephant expert. I am simply curious beyond reason. This book would not have been possible without the help of many of the world's leading elephant and captive wildlife professionals, elephant experts, animal advocates, and individuals closely associated with the featured elephants. The following people guided me on my quest to understand more about elephant captivity in general and about Stoney in particular. Much of the information cited in this book comes from their work.

The person at the top of the list to thank is Las Vegas-based animal advocate Linda Faso. Through dozens of conversations, she has provided invaluable advice and information as well as her point of view. Quite simply, it could not have happened without her. Pat Derby of the Performing Animal Welfare Society (PAWS), likewise, has been equally patient and priceless in sharing her experiences during Stoney's last year of life. She and Ed Stewart were gracious hosts during the conferences hosted at their 2,300 acre elephant and tiger sanctuary near Sacramento, California, in the springs of 2009 and 2010. In a sense, this book largely chronicles Linda and Pat's experience trying to help Stoney.

I am also extremely grateful for Sally Joseph's insight and input regarding her years living with and caring for Stoney. After all, she was with the elephant daily for more than a decade. My several editors were instrumental in encouraging me to think more systematically. Other people have directly contributed to this project, and I thank them all deeply and sincerely.

Many experts, advocates, and circus performers gave their time to help this curious unknown writer learn about some of the complexities of the elephant performance world. When I began, I was certain it was a black and white issue. With their input and guidance, I now understand it is not. As one legendary animal advocate told me, "it's not always about right or wrong. It's often more about perspective."

This book is a historical examination of the two elephants, Mary at the beginning of the twentieth century and Stoney at its close. Various arguments are represented, but this book is not about blame; it is about gathering information and knowledge in order to understand a subject. As mentioned, the issue of elephant captivity is not black or white. It is much more elusive and complex than many people will acknowledge. I am honored that so many professionals and world-renowned experts were willing to meet and talk with me in my effort to tell Stoney's story, among them:

Dr. Cythia Moss, Dr. Joyce Poole, Carol Buckley, Dr. Thomas Hartgrove, Dr. Vandana Shiva, Dr. Elliot Katz, Captain Paul Watson, Don Elroy, Debbie Leahy, Doris Lin, Ingrid Newkirk, Lisa Lange, the great Bob Barker, Ric O'Barry, Mark Berman, Dr. Karen Davis, Dr. Marc Bekoff, Dr. G.A. Bradshaw, and—undoubtedly—others whom, to my future horror, I have failed to list. The following animal advocacy groups have all graciously endorsed this book even though I am a member of none of them:

The Performing Animal Welfare Society, The Amboseli Trust for Elephants, Sea Shepherd Conservation Society, People for the Ethical Treatment of Animals, The Earth Island Institute, United Poultry Concerns, Elephant Voices, Animal Defenders International, In Defense of Animals, Born Free Foundation, Keiko.com, SHARK (Showing Animals Respect and Kindness), The Las Vegas Society for the Prevention of Cruelty to Animals, Action for Animals: Oakland, People Against Cruelty to Animals: Las Vegas, Stoney's Voice, and Chattanooga Animal Advocates.

My family has been very supportive of my rambling path, my incessant woods walking. My wife, Erin, is my sensible anchor in life, and her joy has sustained me on this years-long and often depressing quest of writing this book. She was many times a beacon in my unending night. She has my appreciation and my love, both without limit. Finally, my mother has been an inspirational example of how to deal with adversity, and I thank her for her quiet and graceful guidance. Writing this book has been difficult. I walked away from the project, completely disowning it on three separate occasions. I solemnly swore I was finished with the whole mess of it. *I don't have time for this*, I told my late-night mirrored face. Three times I quit.

But I couldn't quit Stoney; he wouldn't go away. He kept standing quietly and staring at me up through the long years, asking who would tell his story. Much more information is out there if you are interested in elephant captivity in the United States. It is a complex subject. There are compelling arguments supporting it and opposing it. This book chronicles only the story of two elephants and the people involved. It is but one source, one point of view. I hope you enjoy it, seek out other perspectives, and make your own decisions.

-M. Jaynes

Part I

Stoney: A Creature of Great Worth

"Ours is not a caravan of despair."
-Rumi

Chapter 1

Elephants and Humans

This book is about two elephants, Stoney and Big Mary.

In 1995, Stoney the Elephant died behind a Las Vegas hotel and casino after an eleven-month medical confinement in a windowless warehouse. In 1916, a circus owner executed Big Mary for killing a man by hanging her from a railroad derrick. This book details their stories, particularly that of Stoney.[1]

Animals entertain us, and sometimes they pay for our sins. Humanity has a long history of interaction with animals, and elephants are no exception. Humans have killed elephants in extraordinary ways. We have hanged elephants. We have electrocuted them. We have gunned and cut them down. We have run them down with trains and buses. We have exploded them with land mines and destroyed them with wartime napalm. For millennia, they have died in captivity from disease, overwork, and torture.

Many people claim to like elephants, and public interest in their stories tends to run high. Too often public awareness of elephants is superficial, informed not by fact but by the caricatures of these animals as presented in entertainment. Because of this fetishizing, we have pressed elephants into service where we can see them and be around them. From Julius Caesar's Rome to the current elephant displays in traveling circuses and zoos, it is apparent humans enjoy these animals. Their grandeur draws us; their greatness intoxicates. Much too frequently, our interest occurs at their expense.

Very few people know of Stoney the Elephant, and a full-length work has never centered on him until now. Understanding what happened to him and his trainer is not an easy task. This book is largely an attempt to equitably document and understand what happened to Stoney and his trainer. After years of research, I feel an affinity for them both.

And I still can't believe what happened.

Chapter 2

Birth and Early Years

Stoney was an Asian elephant born on June 17, 1973, at Portland's Oregon Zoo, also known as the Metro Washington Park Zoo. The zoo transferred Stoney when he was less than a year old to animal trainer Ken Chisholm and a children's zoo in Montreal.[1] From there, the respected animal trainers Mike and Sally LaTorres bought Stoney for $6,500 from the Hunt Brothers International Animal Exchange, keeping him for the remainder of his life.

In the wild, male elephants often stay with their mothers for up to eight years, and females remain in the herd under the guidance of a matriarch for life. Male elephants, or bulls, leave the herd during adolescence and spend the majority of their lives as semi-solitary animals, though kinship bull-packs do loosely form.

We know a fair amount about Stoney's family. He was part of a group of sixteen captive-born elephants between the bull Thonglaw and other cows, including Stoney's mother. In 1947, a trapper caught Thonglaw in the wild when the elephant was a very young Cambodian juvenile. Berry then transferred Thonglaw to the Seattle Woodland Park Zoo and then to the Portland Zoo, where he sired Stoney and many other elephants. Thonglaw died at the age of 27 during an operation under anesthesia the year after Stoney's birth.

In indigenous ranges, elephants can live more than sixty years, and for reasons not completely understood captive elephants often live much shorter lives than their free-living counterparts do. In 2004, the average life expectancy of captive Asian and African elephants in the United States was 44.8 and 43.3, respectively, though some have lived quite longer. An Asian elephant once lived to age 86.[2]

Another elephant trapper caught Stoney's mother, Pet, in Thailand in 1959. She was also transferred to Seattle Woodland Park and then to the Portland Zoo, where she lived for many years. She suffered from degenerative arthritis, a very common demise of zoo elephants caused (among other things) by standing on concrete (Elephants should always be standing on dirt floors, according to Dr. Elliot Katz of In Defense of Animals). The zoo euthanized her on August 2, 2006, at the age of 51. Stoney's parents did their part to contribute to their species' rapidly decreasing gene pool.

In addition to Stoney, Pet birthed four other elephants between 1963 and 1982. She also gave birth to another one in 1991 that lived only one day. The online Elephant Database lists for him neither a name nor a cause of death. Stoney's maternal siblings who survived birth include Dino, Judy, Sung-Surin (also called Shine), and Teak, (also called Rajah). Information regarding them is available at the Elephant Database. Stoney's father also sired other elephants at the zoo.[3]

After Mike and Sally LaTorres bought Stoney, he soon began training for their animal act. They were nice people, it was a very small operation, and Stoney was the only performing elephant. Sally was married to Mike and was with Stoney from the time the couple received him in 1976 until their divorce when Stoney was thirteen. Very little information is available regarding where Stoney performed around the country or how he spent the winter months.[4] Nonetheless, a somewhat grainy picture of Stoney's early years has been pieced together.

Chapter 3

The Easy Years: 1973-1986

Some animal trainers are abusive, but generalizations are unproductive. Sally LaTorres is a pertinent example. When Sally and Mike received Stoney in the mid-seventies, there were not many elephant trainers in the United States. Many of them routinely utilized practices that many of today's professionals consider excessively forceful. In fact, the best elephant performers in the business trained Sally and Mike.[1] Techniques of dominance training, such as chaining and the use of bull-hooks (a controversial fireplace poker-like tool also known as an *ankus* or a *guide*), were commonplace and still are in many places. The trainers taught Mike and Sally to deprive elephants of food in order to stave off musth, a period of sexual aggression in bulls that makes them difficult to control. It was because of their skill in applying these techniques that Mike and Sally LaTorres were respected animal trainers.

Though many believe elephants should not be used in performance, advocates of the practice point out that the practice of elephant training has made advances. Some no longer employ the brutal methods often depicted on undercover training videos.[2] Sally LaTorres now believes the methods she learned were flawed and no longer supports them. In fact, she is an advocate of non-dominance training and has become an animal advocate. At any rate, in the seventies elephant trainers largely believed that the only way to keep an audience safe was to establish complete dominance over the elephant. This involved dominance training with bull-hooks and other brutal techniques.

The animal advocacy group Born Free, USA defines bull-hooks on its Website:

> The bull-hook is a training device used to train and control elephants. It is also called an ankus, elephant goad, or elephant hook. The handle is made of wood, metal, or other substantial material. At one end is a sharp steel hook and poker, similar to the shape of a fireplace poker. Both ends of the bull-hook are used to inflict damage. The hook is used to apply varying degrees of pressure to sensitive spots on an elephant's body, causing the elephant to move away from the source of discomfort. When the hooked end is held, the handle can be used as a club, inducing substantial pain when the elephant is struck in areas where little tissue separates skin and bone.

Surprisingly, the skin of elephants, though apparently rough and thick, is as sensitive as human skin. Elephant trainers still debate the use of the bull-hook. Many believe it is necessary to establish control of the large animals and does not require forceful application, while others believe the tool is abusive. Despite the fierce debate, bull-hook use remains a standard practice with many trainers. The subject is complicated.

Sally says if she had known then what she knows now, Stoney would have had a much better life. However, at the time, she continues, they were simply ignorant. In fact, many elephant trainers, mahouts, and keepers proclaim a great love for the animals under their supervision. Surely many have the elephant's best interest at heart. Some—perhaps even most—truly love the animals. This is certainly true of Sally, who has always loved Stoney deeply. It also seemed that Stoney cared for Mike and Sally in kind.

Sally was essentially Stoney's mother. He was barely three years old when they got him. Many elephants in the wild nurse up to two or three years of age, and Stoney was completely dependent upon his new family for all his needs. Stoney quickly bonded with Sally, whose role as primary caregiver meant she saw to his social needs, while Mike filled the roles of both trainer and showman. To Sally and Mike, Stoney was a son. Mike cared very much for Stoney, but it was Sally who would most often visit with him and take him on walks and let him graze throughout the five-acre property the couple lived on during those halcyon years. Mike tended to be more reserved in his expression of affection for Stoney while Sally beamed and crooned.

A souvenir program documents Stoney's earliest known circus appearance. It is a program and coloring book for the International All-Star Circus managed by Nordmark and Hood Presentations in Sarasota, Florida. It features a very young Stoney performing with Mike. Stoney's act description reads, with alternate spelling, "Stonie: Mike LaTorres presents that peerless Pasha of Pachyderm presentation and his Indian elephant. Literally a ton of fun." Page two of the handbill features three pictures of a very young Stoney performing three tricks. The handbill is not dated, but Stoney appears to be no more than four or five years old. This provides an approximate date of 1977. In the pictures, Stoney, sporting diminutive tusks and a headband, sits on his haunches. In another, he performs an elevated front leg stand, while the third shows him in a headstand. The couple trained Stoney early and put him to the stage with little delay. The headline on the page reads, "Clear the Way! Here Comes Baby Stonie."

The program features several human and animal acts. After intermission, the program touts "Uncle Heavy's Pork Chop Review," which featured "the only trained, performing pigs being presented anywhere today." The second half of the show featured clowns, trapeze artists, balancing acts, a unicycle act, and an escape by an artist from a locked trunk. The "Vasques

Chimps" are held up as "the cutest of circus babies," but it is Stoney who is the last act, the grand finale. Elephants, even young ones, have been the stars of the show from the earliest years of the traveling circus. Early circuses were judged based on two things: how many cars they had in their trains, and how many elephants they had in their shows. The more elephants a circus had, the more grandeur and respect it commanded.

As Stoney neared his teenage years, he performed at circuses, Renaissance fairs, children's parks, and other venues. It remained most often Sally who would visit with him, walk him, and tell him he was loved. For over a decade, she slept mere yards from the elephant each night. Stoney slept in the rear of the semi-trailer, and the couple slept in the front. There was a pass-through, and Sally would spend many hours listening to him sleep or eat.

The shows continued for years as Stoney grew larger. Sally was a part of the act, and later in Stoney's life she is featured in several publicity shots along with the elephant and LaTorres. In one photo, Stoney stands on his back legs, and Sally sits proudly atop his neck. She never came to complete terms with the fact that Mike insisted Stoney do the hind-leg stand trick as well as the hind-leg walk. Even at thirteen, Stoney did not like it. She says he would always rise into the hind-leg walk hesitantly. She had less of a problem with the back-leg stand, since he was young and did those easily. Mike eventually insisted on the hind-leg walk since it was a standard trick in elephant acts and he wanted to be profitable. At that point, both Sally and Stoney complained. The discussions got very heated, and the walk was never easy for Stoney.

Elephant trainers and performers often claim that some elephants really do enjoy performing while some do not. Of course it may be impossible to judge enjoyment, but some elephants require much less manipulation to learn and perform the tricks. Some elephants take to it and at least appear to enjoy the routines, while some do not cooperate and seem to loathe the ring. Sally reports that Stoney did not love to perform, but he did not always hate it either. He spent many hours of traveling days inside his trailer with very little activity, and at least performing was exercise. If nothing else, perhaps performances helped Stoney stretch his legs.

Critics of the industry often cite isolation and inadequate space as two dominant issues with elephant performance. In some cases, there is brutality to consider. Other than occasionally, Stoney did not often require physical discipline, though invariably Mike was the disciplinarian. Sally points out that Mike was never aggressively violent with Stoney. Stoney simply didn't require much punishment. He was cooperative and easygoing. The physical discipline administered to Stoney generally was not harsh. As Sally says, Stoney was a good boy and always behaved well for her and Mike. There were brutal elephant trainers at that time on the American circus circuit; Mike LaTorres was not one of them.

Stoney very much seemed to enjoy giving children's rides. These rides usually occurred in a parking lot or a field near a fairground, the children waiting impatiently for their turn to climb on his back in wonderment. It was a leisurely way for the LaTorres family, including Stoney, to pass an afternoon. Sally fondly remembers spending hours sitting next to Stoney on the ride platform, his trunk wrapped affectionately around her leg or arm. Stoney would often nap on cooler days or if it were raining. During the rain, Sally would put a blanket or rain tarp on his back and sit under him. Mike, easygoing and likeable, enjoyed talking to the attendees and answering questions about Stoney in the afternoon sun.

What the elephant seemed to enjoy the most, however, were the many Renaissance fairs in and around Colorado that they would attend when Stoney was a preteen. This generally involved getting Stoney into period garb and simply standing around or walking peacefully through the fairgrounds while people petted or fed him. This was by far Stoney's favorite work, and people always reacted kindly toward him. Sally pointed out that during the years she was with Stoney, they never failed a single USDA inspection, and Stoney was properly fed and cared for, according to the standards of the time. Indeed, research verified her claim.

Life was not always work for Stoney, at least not year round. During the winter off-season, the couple and Stoney lived on a fenced five-acre property in Florida complete with an elephant barn. Times during these winter months were mostly good ones. Stoney would help Sally build fences on their property, passing rails to his family with his trunk, and he liked to play with Sally's dog, a Border Collie named Travis who became his close friend. While building fences, Stoney would often get distracted by the ponies the couple also had on the property and playfully chase them about. An elephant can definitely pose hazards, but due to his easygoing manner and calm demeanor, they never worried about his wandering the property. Sally tended to her fence building, always confident in Stoney's playful, nonviolent nature.

Mike had a dog too, a Rottweiler-Labrador mix named Maggie, but it was Travis the Border Collie of whom Stoney was especially fond. Those years were not perfect for the couple or Stoney, but during the nights, Travis would often sit or sleep between Stoney's legs, perched in the rear of the semi-trailer where Stoney slept, both of them content. Things seemed good, and it seemed they would always be.

The fact that Stoney bonded so closely with Travis is not a surprise. As do most highly intelligent animals, elephants need close familial and kinship bonds due to their great need for socialization. A leading expert on captive elephants and founder of the first elephant sanctuary in the United States, Pat Derby, reports[3] that when elephants in captive single situations are deprived of sociality, the elephant's need for familial connections is so paramount that it will bond with "just about anything on four legs." She has seen solitary elephants bond with dogs, goats, and even donkeys. Stoney's need for elephantine companionship was never met, but he found a connection with Travis.

In Florida, Sally, Stoney, Travis, and Mike would take long walks, and Sally often would sit in a swing on the property and let Stoney go off-leash, free to graze and wander around being an elephant in the afternoon sun. Sometimes Stoney and Travis would go off by themselves and explore the fenced five acres. As much as she could, Sally gave Stoney time off his chains.

The famous Renaissance fair in Larkspur, Colorado, was one of Sally's favorite recurring gigs. This particular fair was perfect since they only worked weekends in the lovely countryside with nothing but nature surrounding them. During downtime during the Larkspur festival, Stoney, the dogs, and Sally would wander in the woods and enjoy the sunshine. Stoney would graze and knock over small trees and eat them. (Elephants in their indigenous habitats display this same tree destroying behavior.) She would find a nice patch of sun, and Stoney would wander and explore the area, always curious and kind. He never went far and frequently reported back to check on Sally before heading out again in another direction. Sally and Stoney would wander through woods as often as they could. Like other elephants, Stoney loved the water. Finding a creek or a pool was a grand occasion, and the elephant usually made a great mess of everything.

In several phone conversations and email interviews, she shared more memories of the off time on the five acres in Florida. It is easy to think of Stoney as her son as she reports the stories. When they were back at the property, Sally would take Stoney out to help her do certain chores. He would putter around and graze while she did various farm work. Stoney was a very steady animal. He preferred to be within sight of her, Mike, or Travis.

Another year they worked a Renaissance fair in Miami at the

site of the old Key Biscayne Zoo, which had moved to its new facility in Homestead not long before. At the festival, the elephant barn, yard, and canal-fed, water-filled moat were still available. Stoney spent much time playing in the five-foot-deep moat, which had many interesting items at the bottom. Stoney would dunk down, dig something up, pull it out of the water, and hold it up as if he had received the Stanley cup. He would hold it way up over his head and then toss it to shore. Usually Stoney only pulled up logs and tires. One time, he pulled up a tricycle and played with it for a while as the afternoon sun moved lower in the western sky.

Sally's maternal bond with Stoney was deep. She often preferred the company of her dogs and Stoney to people, so she spent most of her free time with them. She knew Stoney's movements and body language, even how to decipher the different looks in his intelligent eyes. They could read each other's mood. She only made this connection, she believes, by living with him day in and day out. She says of this daily contact:

> One of my big arguments with zoo people is that there is not a lot of opportunity at zoos with overtime and understaffing to learn about elephants by actually living with them and spending hours, days, and years watching and learning their behavior. Zoo people who think they can develop a deep bond with their elephants by working with them a couple of hours a day, five days a week, are often proven wrong, sometimes in a very painful way.

She values the decade she spent with her Stoney, "her good boy," as she still calls him. Her time with him provided Sally keen insight on elephants that helped her continue her work with animals after the good days ended.

Her experience also turned her into an advocate, provoking her to explore and, eventually, to advocate strongly *protected contact*. Protected contact, according to the elephant expert Dan Koehl's elephant database, is "sometimes referred to as a more humane method of manipulating elephants in captivity, since the free contact system more or less relies on the fact that the elephant is to be dominated by the trainer, like it does with an animal higher in rank within the elephant group." In protected contact, trainers are always behind grates and bars, and humans never walk freely among elephants. There are advocates of both free and protected contact, but virtually all circus elephant training is free contact. It is protected contact, or "PC," that Sally Joseph, along with the Performing Animal Welfare Society (PAWS), The Tennessee Elephant Sanctuary, The Detroit Zoo, The Oakland Zoo, and others, overwhelmingly advocate. However, within the arena of elephant performance, the debate continues. Trainers have employed free contact for many centuries, and many people in the industry believe it is the preferred method as it establishes a closer bond between elephant and trainer due to the contact and the tactile nature of elephant communication.

Sally and Mike's marriage worsened, declined, and ended. When Sally knew she had to take care of herself and leave LaTorres, the thought of leaving Stoney behind was torturous. Who would make sure he got off leash? Would Mike give him proper care and attention? Who would listen to him sleep and love him? Travis was coming with her, so could Maggie, the Lab/Rottweiler mix, fill that gap? These answers were all unknown to her. Mike was not a bad person toward Stoney, but she believed his affection toward the elephant was less outwardly pronounced than hers. She didn't think Mike would neglect Stoney, but she didn't know for certain; thus her agony. Desperate, she examined the possibility of taking Stoney with her, but she was destitute and it was impossible. Finally, in 1986, during the thirteenth year of Stoney's life, she had to leave, taking Travis with her in her Toyota pickup. The parting was bitter, and she still carries a significant burden for Stoney and his long journey into night. Though her situation offered no alternatives, she partially blames herself. She believes she was the only mother he ever knew. How was she to accept leaving her good boy, her son, her irreplaceable Stoney?

The couple separated, and Sally filed for divorce. Mike never responded, and the judge awarded Sally the dissolution on January 27, 1986. No longer would she take Travis and Stoney on long walks or build fences under the winter sun. No longer would they live closely together in the special bond of the tight-knit peripatetic family barely getting by and facing the unknown future. No longer would they sleep near each other, sharing anxieties and taking nourishment from shared love and the closeness of each other's body heat, the small reassurances of steady night breathing. Given the elephant's accurately famed memory, it is likely he remembered those good times for the rest of his life, or, at least, it was possible for him to do so. At the time of separation, however, Sally was distraught and had no idea what would come next for her or Stoney. The carefree days of woods-walking, creek-splashing, and tricycle-tossing came to an end for Sally. She went her way, and Mike and Stoney stayed on the road. She has never gotten over it. Sally saw Stoney only one last time after the divorce, briefly, in 1988. Sally was beyond distraught. She had no idea what would come next for her, or for the elephant she had to leave behind.

Chapter 4

The Lost Years: 1986–1994

With Sally gone, Stoney began touring the country with Mike. I would like to note that LaTorres is deceased, and as a result, the following events were reconstructed from the public record in good faith to the best of my ability without the benefit of his input. Once the elephant reached his teenage years, LaTorres often kept him on short rations to make him easier to control. Again, this was standard practice. The show went on, and Stoney began appearing in the public record. The first known USDA documented performance occurred when Stoney appeared at the Wondercade in May of 1982. A picture taken during this stint can be found on page 43 of the Circus Historical Society's journal, *Bandwagon*.[1] In it, a young, small-tusked Stoney wearing a headdress stands beside LaTorres in a showman's exaggerated tuxedo, bull-hook in hand. Inspection reports and health certificates document various places LaTorres and Stoney appeared. For people who take an interest in the details of Stoney's life, these are invaluable. The earliest obtained report is dated two years before the couple's divorce. This has a nine-year-old Stoney entertaining at a Delaware Shrine Circus along with Mike and Sally in April and May of 1984. In 1987, the USDA inspected Stoney at LaTorres' five-acre residence in central Florida, and all was in order. Another year passed with no documented appearances or violations. No news is good news.

Reports then document that Stoney appeared at a fair ground in Massachusetts in May of 1987 and a Shrine Circus in Wilkes-Barre Pennsylvania in March of 1988. Stoney wintered at the

Florida quarters and presumably entertained where and when Mike could find employment for them. Information regarding the years of Stoney's life between Sally's departure and the first United States Department of Agriculture's Animal and Plant Health Inspection Service (USDA-APHIS)[2] inspection violations is available, but it is sparse. From the time he was four until he was twenty-one, Stoney performed around the country and in Canada at venues including Quebec's Cirque Universal, several Shriners' Circuses, and the Tommy Hanneford Circus. Several Renaissance fairs in Colorado and quite a few roadside shows all featured Stoney during this time. Beyond these exist some known appearances, but there must be many undocumented ones since the act was Mike's primary means of making a living.

Stoney and LaTorres continued working and touring. In March of 1989, they performed at Shriner Circuses in Grand Rapids, Michigan, and Indianapolis, Indiana. During the first half of 1990, at age seventeen, Stoney toured with the Tommy Hanneford Circus. This engagement brought him through Greenville, South Carolina; Little Rock, Arkansas; Dallas and Houston Texas; and Tampa Bay, Florida along with other stops. Also in 1990, the USDA-APHIS inspected Stoney in Kansas, Missouri, Arkansas, and Illinois. A busy year. Stoney also performed in Vidbel's Olde Tyme Circus during June of 1990. February of 1991 documents another Shriner Circus in Flint, Michigan, and three months later another Shriner Circus and Road Show stint brought Stoney back through Houston, Texas, as well as Dayton and Cincinnati, Ohio. He was nineteen years old at these stops.

Stoney and Mike appeared in a Shrine Circus in Warrensville Heights, Ohio, in September 1990. They also traveled with the Royal Hanneford Circus in 1991 and appeared at the Jolly Roger Park in Ocean City, Maryland, in May 1991. Other documented stops include a circus in Greenwood, South Carolina in February 1992; a road show in Flint and Saginaw, Michigan in 1992; and

The Lost Years: 1986–1994

several road shows with various unlisted stops in 1993.

The serious USDA-APHIS non-compliance issues began in 1992.[3] The agency inspections revealed several issues on February 27 of that year. The inspector found excess algae in Stoney's water trough, determined that Stoney was underweight, and found that he had no access to shade when not in his transport trailer. The 1992 violation—the first of five—merits a detailed digression. The primary concern of the inspector's report is Stoney's weight. He writes that "this 18 yr. old male Asian elephant is quite thin. Mr. LaTorres stated that Stoney had been given a diet of two and a half to three bales of hay with supplements since Oct. 1991 to prevent musth." LaTorres told the inspector that he had used nutrient restriction to control musth in the past, but claimed that Stoney had been put back on his regular diet (of unknown foods). His weight was the paramount concern, though it was not the only one.

The inspector ordered LaTorres to consult Stoney's attending veterinarian immediately to develop and document a diet that would bring Stoney back to a healthy weight. He gave LaTorres two weeks to mail a copy of the plan to the sector office. The inspector's instructions expressly prohibit LaTorres from using food deprivation to sap Stoney's virile strength as part of his overall care and handling strategy. He specifies that Stoney's "handling method must not cause stress, physical harm, or unnecessary discomfort. Food deprivation shall not be used to train, work or otherwise handle the animal."

LaTorres' response framed the issue in terms of handling Stoney. He claimed, in accordance with his training, that periodic food deprivation was necessary to keep him handle-able. The final report is adamant: "as of this date something other than forced food deprivation shall be used to control musth and/or Stoney's behavior." It is not known exactly what was implemented. The USDA's role in monitoring performing animals through its APHIS arm is to provide guidance to the exhibitors who care for them and perform with them. From this example, it seems clear that at least some exhibitors such as LaTorres could benefit from closer oversight and more guidance regarding the seriousness of non-compliance violations as well as the implementation of more fines and citations. If the only method of musth control Mike knew of was food deprivation in his experience, perhaps the USDA-APHIS could have suggested alternatives. It appears that at least in writing that it did not.

The 1992 inspector also was concerned about Stoney's skin condition and observed numerous lesions. LaTorres reported some of them were associated with a skin condition triggered by the periods of food reduction. There were patches of crusting, light discoloration, redness, bleeding, abrasions, and other skin loss. Small puncture wounds at the back end of each rear leg oozed small amounts of blood. LaTorres told the inspector he believed these wounds were from his use of a bull-hook on Stoney. The inspector found more lightly bleeding abrasions on Stoney's left shoulder and front surface of his left leg. In response to these conditions, the inspector ordered that a vet assess Stoney's "body weight, general health and skin condition at least every ninety days as of 3-15-92." At the time of this inspection, LaTorres could not produce proper records of documented veterinary care.

The inspection report also notes improper waste disposal. The inspector found that LaTorres was not operating his waste disposal facility properly in a manner that minimizes vermin infestation, odors, and hazardous diseases. Piles of Stoney's manure stood much closer to his main enclosure than regulations allowed. These conditions were especially hazardous because the wounds on Stoney's skin were susceptible to infections. Standing in excrement also can result in foot rot and other disease and discomfort.

The inspector's 1992 report takes issue not merely with the conditions in Stoney's enclosure, but with the enclosure itself.

While Stoney was at LaTorres' home site, he lived in a small travel trailer, which was also found to be in violation. The inspector found it unacceptable, citing both torn wood and broken boards on the doors and sharp metal edges visible on the opposite wall of doors and back walls.

This first detailed inspection report documents that as of February 1992, Stoney was on the USDA-APHIS's radar. These violations are serious, and it seems logical that Mike reflected on them after the inspector left. From the very few first hand reports of him gathered for this book, it can be assumed that LaTorres likely did the best he could in accordance with his knowledge and his station, and they stayed on the road. In the summer of 1993, Tommy Hanneford produced another circus at the Great Escape Amusement Park in Lake George, New York, which featured the act. After this summer, they again most likely wintered in Florida. Stoney's crisscrossing the country in his battered trailer continued until Stoney arrived in the glitz and glamor of Las Vegas in early 1994.

Chapter 5

Las Vegas: The Beginning of the End

Stoney's performing life continued.[1] Las Vegas, Nevada, has become a world-renowned carefree destination for some and the end of the line for others. Joe Oesterle, who has written on the subject of Vegas culture, writes while briefly living in Las Vegas he met more outrageous characters in four months than most people could hope to meet in a lifetime. Vices abound, and the strange city in the desert earns its moniker of "Sin City."

To non-Nevadans, Las Vegas and Reno are the entirety of Nevada; conversely, Nevadans consider Vegas more a suburb of Los Angeles than a part of the Silver State. Expatriated residents from more traditional cities of the Union make it to the city to live a theoretically freer life. The city attracts adventurers, ufologists, conspiracy theorists, spiritual seekers, showgirls, sex workers, gamblers, and the like. Uncounted films and books feature the city as a place offering the well-worn narrative cycle of promise, adventure, disillusionment, and downfall. In Sin City, all bets are off and just about anything can happen.

Casino shows are also ubiquitous and long-respected features of the Las Vegas entertainment industry. While LaTorres and Stoney were touring the country's smaller venues, the Luxor Casino opened in Las Vegas. It was actively searching for a new elephant act for its entertainment lineup, since another elephant act had withdrawn its female elephant from the job due to conditions considered unsuitable (The casino had extremely low ceilings in many of the areas where the elephant often would be).

Though more opulent casinos have since been built, when the

Luxor opened in 1993 it was regarded as a marvel and touted as the eighth wonder of the world. The casino, with an eye toward dazzling guests, sought an elephant act that could provide an air of grandeur to the dinner theater shows. In doing so, they not only stepped onto a path long-trodden and lucrative, but also complicated. An elephant exhibitor has a significant burden to meet in keeping an elephant physically healthy enough to pass USDA-APHIS inspections.

Stoney and his trainer left Florida in late January, 1994, and arrived in Las Vegas on March 1. He and LaTorres auditioned and got the job. The hotel provided housing facilities for Stoney in the form of a USDA-APHIS-inspected-and-approved warehouse-type storage building. Notably, this inspection produced the first USDA-APHIS non-compliance for LaTorres in Las Vegas. The inspector's report dated March 3, 1994, two days following Stoney's arrival, again cites LaTorres for transporting his elephant in a noncompliant trailer. Stoney logged many miles in that trailer, and the trailer made its way into inspectors' logbooks from central Florida to Quebec to Las Vegas. The March 3 allegation was a similar violation Mike had received in January, two months previous. It appears LaTorres failed to act upon the USDA-APHIS orders and that agency officials did not actively enforce them. Stoney's existence in the flashy city was typical of performing elephants. Like most of them, he was led from the performance area to his restricted holding area and did not get to experience the great majority of what elephants enjoy and seek in the wild. At this point, he was twenty-one years old and was undoubtedly accustomed to the rigors of traveling in small circuses, sideshows, and carnivals.

Elephants require proper nutrition to maintain optimal bone health, and Stoney's bones were not in prime condition. When the couple bought Stoney, the seller told Mike and Sally that Stoney's wild-captured father had bone problems and that Stoney would most likely have leg issues as well and would not be ideal for leg-balancing tricks due to his father's condition.[2] The reader may recall Sally LaTorres' dislike of the hind-leg walk. At this point in his career, this trick was taking on a greater element of risk. Circus trainers and spokespeople often report all elephant tricks are purposefully designed extensions of natural behavior, but neither extended nor repeated rear-leg stands nor the hind-leg walk are common behaviors of free-ranging elephants, according to Pat Derby of the Performing Animal Welfare Society. LaTorres commonly ran through these particular tricks many times with Stoney before each performance. Stoney was reluctant to rise into the hind-leg walk ever since the days Sally was with him. He needed motivation to do the trick.

Chapter 6

A Night to Remember

Around eight o'clock in the evening on September 23, 1994, LaTorres was warming up Stoney backstage at the Luxor by having him practice the hind-leg stand. During this practice, Stoney was seriously injured. His left rear hamstring muscle audibly snapped. An eyewitness reported that when the tendon snapped, the elephant began screaming and dropped to his knees. There were many people around, such as stagehands and dancers, and they all heard the elephant's turmoil. The injury was very serious, and Stoney needed immediate veterinary care. LaTorres and officials from the Luxor helped him as much as they could. After a vet injected him with morphine, the assembled crew helped Stoney into a dumpster (the only handy thing sturdy enough to support him). Then they moved the dumpster via forklift to the stable behind the hotel. This is documented to have taken over six hours.

The injury is also well-documented.[1] One of Stoney's vets, Dr. Martin R. Dinnes, reports the injury caused "the complete rupture of his left rear gastrocnemius tendon," a terribly painful injury to bear. Of course, the elephant could not stand or walk very well and is reported to have forcefully and often vocalized pain during the six-and-a-half hours it took to get him from the practice area to the holding shed behind the hotel. A Luxor security report discusses the events of that night. It indicates that no photos were taken and no evidence was collected. This was, most likely, common procedure, and it appears the enlisted workers really wanted to help Stoney and Mike as much as they could. Few are unresponsive to the suffering of an elephant.

Perhaps the events of this night signify more than the eventual five detailed USDA-APHIS citations, the vet reports, and the ensuing trial, that a single individual of limited means, no matter how kind and well-meaning, is most likely ill-equipped to care properly for an elephant. This continues to be debated, but the requisite upkeep to care properly for a captive elephant is financially, mentally, and physically significant, and it is hard to imagine an individual of limited means who could be prepared to provide for an elephant. In the world of captive elephants, when things go bad, they can go very bad. The individual elephant exhibitor could easily become overwhelmed if circumstances are not ideal. Stoney's injury was a very bad one.

The security guard provides detailed handwritten notes regarding the six-hour ordeal. He reports that at approximately 11:10 pm he was walking through the loading dock area when he saw LaTorres, whom he knew to be performing in the "Winds of the Gods" show as Stoney's trainer. Mike told him Stoney hurt his leg while practicing, and he needed help getting Stoney to his barn. The guard contacted his supervisor and apprised him of the situation. LaTorres also requested the hotel contact a veterinarian. Several security officers and the supervisor began attempting to contact vets. They tried the Mirage, a hotel known for its exotic animal acts, which at the time included an elephant show. At 11:30 pm two more people arrived on the scene with the desire to help out, including an engineer and one Mr. Peter Jackson.

At two minutes before one in the morning, approximately four hours after the time of the incident, local vet Dr. Thomas Hartgrove arrived. He writes that on that night he "was presented with a 21 year old Asian bull elephant named 'Stoney.' The elephant had collapsed while doing a hind-leg stand. They had moved him approximately 100 yards under his own power into the parking lot when I arrived."[2] Hartgrove's examination revealed:

The elephant was three-legged lame on his left hind leg. No crepitus was felt on manipulation and there was swelling inside and behind his stifle. Blood work revealed high levels of CPK (an enzyme associated with muscle damage). Based on these findings a diagnosis of soft tissue injury was made.

After examining the elephant, he ordered three grams of morphine for immediate injection for pain management. Stoney was lying in the parking lot at this point, likely in considerable pain. The security supervisor and other officers immediately began calling local pharmacies to locate the required morphine and found one on West Sahara Avenue. Someone promptly left with Dr. Hartgrove's prescription to retrieve the medication.

The incident report continues with an entry at 2:55 am. LaTorres was able to walk the medicated Stoney very slowly into an open-wheeled dumpster, the only handy thing sturdy enough to transport a young adult male Asian elephant. At 3:50 am the *ad hoc* team secured Stoney in his quarters. The report states "Stoney was safe and sound in the stables at 0350 hrs." Therefore, although everyone at the scene worked as quickly as they seemed to be able, it took approximately seven hours to get Stoney from the site of his injury to his barn. One does not simply carry an elephant to the vet in the back seat of one's car.

Other accounts of the accident exist. One such account is the USDA-APHIS summary of events regarding the operation of LaTorres' Las Vegas site from February 1994 to August 1995. The report's author is Animal Care Inspector Greg Wallen, who eventually witnessed Stoney's death. The report, dated August 31, 1995, reads:

On September 23, 1994 the animal [Stoney] was involved in a mishap at the showroom, backstage, prior to an evening performance. For reasons unknown, the animal fell while doing a hind-leg stand and injured his left hind leg. The attending vet was contacted immediately. He supervised the animal's movement from the hotel back to the holding barn. The animal was examined, tests were conducted and treatments and medications were prescribed.

This truncated account lacks many of the details in the security report. Wallen's report states a vet "was contacted immediately." The security report places the arrival of Dr. Hartgrove at two minutes shy of 1.00 am, some hours after the initial injury. Wallen's report cites "reasons unknown" for the accident. However, it seems likely that the repeated forced practice of the rear hind-leg stand is the reason Stoney's tendon ruptured. As noted before, Stoney resisted performing the trick for many years and according to numerous experts[3] it is possible with bull-hook dominance training to overcome elephants' resistance to many tricks. Of course, Wallen was most likely unaware of this.

From the injury on September 23, Stoney could not stand or walk very well, and keeping his weight on the injured leg would only aggravate the injury. As a result, Dr. Hartgrove designed a makeshift sling to support him until a more permanent solution could be located. A dancer in the show at the time was there on September 23. He provides insight regarding the sling support device:

> I did visit Stoney after the accident and it was very sad. It almost looked like he was enjoying the sling because he would rock himself back and forth like he was playing. I think it was something like a span-set material that riggers use to hang heavy equipment, which was covered in a soft cloth. But, the sling was chafing him because he would swing himself all the time...The shrieks he made that evening were so heart breaking. I remember it took them all night just to get him up

the ramp from the arena to his housing.[4]

Dr. Hartgrove soon deemed the sling unsuitable due to this chafing. Eight days after the injury on October 1, 1994, he placed Stoney inside a crush he designed, procured the materials for, and built himself in Stoney's barn. A crush is a mechanical rehabilitative device utilized to keep cattle and other large animals upright when they cannot stand. A crush immobilizes, to some degree, the animal in order to keep it from aggravating injuries. Stoney's innovative crush was a custom-designed affair specifically for the treatment of his injury. Stoney's recovery was always uncertain, but the Luxor officials demanded he receive proper vet care. Stoney had the full support of Mike and the hotel, so Dr. Hartgrove soon decided against euthanasia. Instead, he prescribed a comprehensive course of physical therapy to give Stoney a fighting chance. Leg injuries to elephants are critically dangerous due to their massive weight. With a proper physical therapy regimen fully implemented, Stoney may have been able to overcome this injury. In early October, 1994, Hartgrove secured Stoney into the metal crush for support and treatment, and his long night began.

Chapter 7

Isolation

October wheeled by, and November arrived. Now things get complicated, and this point in the story is where the unfortunate blame game most often begins. This book is not about blame; upcoming chapters will address this in more detail.

Elephants are very tactile and closely knit within their family groups. They are social animals requiring close guidance from older members of the herd. This guidance is not limited to the mother; the whole herd often provides input for babies and juveniles that benefit from many aunts, so to speak. Asian and African elephants enjoy stable and active social interactions led by a matriarch. The males leave the herds after adolescence, only contacting female herds in the future to mate. Bull elephants do, however, form homosocial friendships with other bulls in small kinship groups. When considering issues involving captivity, the social aspect of elephants cannot be overemphasized. A 2005 study reports that African savannah elephants spend up to 80 percent of their time together, behave in coordinated manners, and display group-coordinated behavior when caring for their young, gathering resources, and providing defense. Family units, kinship groups, and larger clans can often consist of up to one hundred elephants, and these closely interacting members help each other out during dry seasons and other times of distress.[1]

Communication is also central to the lives of wild elephants, both Asian and African. Research suggests that these intelligent, long-lived animals may have long-since adapted the capacity to transmit information across generations.[2] While they still do not completely understand the behavior, some researchers argue that intergenerational communication influences a great deal of elephant behavior. Some have observed that the wariness some elephant families exhibit toward humans may be based on information passed from one generation to the next. It is not hard to imagine the strain a solitary existence could put on such social animals. Sally LaTorres did a commendable job seeing to Stoney's needs during his younger years, but even the most well-meaning owners rarely have the means to provide a proper habitat, which requires many acres of open range. When Stoney was installed in his windowless barn, his isolation and lack of movement may have replaced his leg injury as his biggest physical and psychological problem. With each passing week and month, Stoney's situation grew direr. The crush was intended as a temporary device to help him keep his weight off his injured hind leg while it healed with the application of daily physical therapy. It was imperative, according to Dr. Hartgrove, that Stoney receive proper physical therapy and get out of the crush as soon as possible. His initial prognosis was that the elephant might have to stay in the crush for up to six months at the absolute most.

Stoney's crush involved a metal bar system with some canvas material that helped support the massive bulk of his weight. The prescribed physical therapy would have involved his putting more and more weight on his injured leg each day while receiving certain massages and medications and performing small exercises. The device was rehabilitative in nature, designed and built by Dr. Hartgrove, and was quite helpful for the situation.

A group of Las Vegas activists kept around-the-clock vigil outside Stoney's shed during the latter months of his isolation. Leading the charge was PAWS, founded in 1984 by former Hollywood animal trainer and author Pat Derby and her partner, Ed Stewart. Since the early seventies, she has advocated only positive reinforcement animal training. Throughout her expansive Hollywood animal training career, Pat never employed domination-training tactics on animals. PAWS maintains three sanctuaries for captive wildlife: thirty acres in Galt, California, one hundred acres (The Amanda Blake Wildlife Refuge) in Herald, California, and 2,300 acres of pristine, natural habitat (ARK 2000) in San Andreas, California. Currently, the ARK 2000 is widely regarded as a leading elephant sanctuary in the United States.[3] It also houses rescued tigers and lions on the property in separate secure locations. The zeal and energy Derby displayed attempting to help Stoney is characteristic of her life, which she has dedicated to animal welfare.

In the seventies, when Mike and Sally were receiving and welcoming Stoney into their Florida lives, Derby trained many exotic animals on the sets of popular television shows, including *Flipper, Lassie, Gunsmoke, Gentle Ben, Daktari,* and many animal films. She also worked as the trainer and spokesperson for the famous Lincoln Mercury car commercial cougars, Chauncey and Christopher. This experience brought her fame and success in the animal training world. During these times, she began developing training methods based on affection and trust instead of fear. Derby's motivation to develop her training method, as she puts it, grew from a sense that her profession was one rampant with neglect and abuse. The first exposé of the violent training methods and minimal care then standard in the entertainment industry was her 1976 autobiography *The Lady and Her Tiger*, which helped launch the American animal rights movement. The book clearly displays she used love and affection to train animals. She writes that she has never hit an elephant with a bull-hook in her life, neither has she beaten an animal. Instead, she employs methods of positive reinforcement. Soon after the publication, Pat met Ed Stewart and retired her performing animals. They remained active in advocating for legislation that would mandate better standards of care and handling for captive wildlife.

Derby and PAWS figure prominently in the last year of Stoney's story. Derby has appeared on many national media programs, including *20/20*, *The Today Show*, and *CBS Evening News*, educating the public on the need to protect wildlife habitat and the dangers of the captive breeding of exotic species. Derby and Stewart developed an elephant handling method that utilizes no bull-hooks, weapons, or adverse training techniques. PAWS was the first organization to use this non-dominance training successfully, and its work has become a model for elephant trainers around the world. PAWS also protects wild species and their habitats with international programs established in India, Mexico, Africa, and Cambodia to diminish human/elephant conflict and to establish protected areas for other wildlife. Like all large organizations, PAWS has its share of detractors; nonetheless, Derby and Stewart work hard to do what they believe to be right. PAWS' greatest concerns are the treatment of animals in traveling shows, animal acts, television, and movies, captive breeding, the exotic animal trade, and inadequate standards of care for all captive wildlife.

The other activist vital to Stoney's story is the independent Vegas-based animal advocate Linda Faso. She was one of the people who kept around-the-clock vigil during Stoney's final months in the barn. She documented daily activities with video, note taking, and spent much time writing to local leaders and attempting to bring the plight of Stoney to the public consciousness. In the national realm of animal advocacy, Faso is well known, and in the world of animal advocacy in Las Vegas, she is legendary, if not the final word. Linda is a diminutive but fiery woman who tells it like it is.

Close friends, Pat and Linda are possibly the two most informed advocates on Earth regarding Stoney and his story. Like others in the field of animal advocacy and animal protection, Linda is unflinching, informed, and eager to state her opinion. A master of public relations, Linda has been instrumental in helping hundreds of animals. Since the eighties, Faso has campaigned for elephants and other animals full time. Two of the elephants currently at the Tennessee Elephant Sanctuary have ties to Vegas, and Faso was instrumental in relocating them. She has also campaigned for numerous animals used in performance, especially big cat acts. Like Derby, there is little doubt Faso will ever quit trying to help animals.

During Stoney's lengthening months in his crush, observers reported the trainer would visit roughly twice a day for about an hour at a time on average, though he would often spend more time with the elephant. Reports from the parent company of the Luxor, Circus Circus Enterprises, however, say the trainer spent much more time with the elephant than that. LaTorres would feed Stoney and give him water by means of a hosepipe, according to PAWS' observers. They believe the parties involved clearly did not fully understand the needs of a captive elephant. For example, when asked why Stoney was not getting any produce, the casino cited a lack of refrigeration capabilities in Stoney's shed, which was mere "yards from a multi-million dollar hotel and casino" as Faso pointedly wrote in her letters. When activists offered to provide produce to the elephant and a refrigerator to LaTorres and the hotel free of charge, the offer was refused. After his visits with Stoney, PAWS' observers headed by Linda Faso noted that the trainer turned off the lights each time he left. No windows in the shed meant Stoney was by himself in the dark on average for about ten to twelve hours a day, by the most conservative estimate if these observations are accurate. Activists were outraged.

It was not only the animal advocates who were enraged at this treatment. When it became more widely known, several veterinary professionals shared their distress regarding Stoney's condition, and their umbrage is well documented. In fact, several things baffled vets regarding LaTorres' handling of the situation.

In Dr. Tom Hartgrove's report dated November 21, 1994 (just under two months following the accident), he notes some of Stoney's skin wounds were healing, but his conditions were not optimal. He reports that he emphatically stressed the need for sawdust to cover the floor and softer protective padding for the belly bar of the crush. Several experts stressed the dire need for padding to protect Stoney from the metal bars of his crush. He was developing gaping pressure sores (similar to bedsores) from constantly rubbing his belly against the metal tubing. Dr. Hartgrove ordered LaTorres to add neoprene padding to the sled, which was a ventral support, also called a "belly bar," which laterally intersected the sides of the crush and provided a place for Stoney to place his stomach, thereby taking weight off his injured leg. The vet also noted a new pressure sore on the left side of Stoney's face, and he clearly expressed concern for the elephant. The notes indicate Stoney's leg was "worse weight bearing." The vet's handwriting looks emphatic, scrawled across the page in urgency. One of his reports dated three weeks earlier displays the same qualities. Scrawled on the side of an itemized bill for services rendered are these words: "Suspect pressure [wound] on face from leaning on crush causing tearing. Need padding. Mike can't or won't locate."

Hartgrove was concerned that Mike might be depressed and lacking adequate finances to take care of the elephant properly. It was unsure if Stoney was receiving the ordered physical therapy. Like other vets who examined Stoney, Dr. Hartgrove was at a loss as to why LaTorres did not follow these simple instructions. Mike had always worked hard at his profession, as Sally reports. Was he now simply lazy and uncaring, or was he suffering from depression and a lack of a wide reaching support system?

Just weeks later on November 28, 1994, another vet expressed similar concerns. Dr. Mike Schmidt of the Asian Elephant Species Survival Program at Portland's Washington Park Zoo (where Stoney was born) examined the elephant. Along with prescribing medications such as Amoxicillin, Naxcel, and Ibuprofen, Dr. Schmidt comments prominently in his report the need for crush padding, which still was not present regardless of Dr. Hartgrove's emphatic suggestion seven days earlier.

Dr. Schmidt sterilized some pressure sores and cultured others. In his November 28 report, Schmidt orders LaTorres to use half-inch neoprene sheets of padding and immediately pad the crush. Dr. Schmidt writes that he "reiterated need to find neoprene" and that "we must get crush padded." Despite the administration of medication by Dr. Hartgrove and other vets, Stoney's pressure sores remained problematic, as veterinarian and USDA-APHIS reports display.[4] Since the ventral belly bar of the crush was never permanently padded, it only added to the pressure sore suffering of Stoney.

Faso located video footage of Stoney in the crush. It is mostly shot from the rear of the elephant. The building appears to be approximately thirty by twenty feet, perhaps slightly larger.[5] It is made of corrugated steel or some other similar material with a rolling garage-type door on one end and an entry door beside it. There are no visible windows. As the camera pans around the dimly lit interior, one sees that the only illumination comes from several overhead fluorescent fixtures in the ceiling. Dominating the small room is the cattle crush with Stoney inside, positioned with his rear to the doors. The crush consists of sidebars of thick steel along with a few uprights and the aforementioned unpadded ventral platform attached to each side of the crush. Stoney repeatedly leans on this during the video, perhaps to get his weight off his injured leg. There appears to be a walkway of approximately six feet surrounding the crush with more room fore and aft. The lighting is poor.

Cattle crushes are not intended to support an animal for large numbers of months. Truly, this hanging isolation was not at all what Dr. Hartgrove envisioned. The crush could have rehabilitated Stoney if things had been different. As the months wore on, after a period of initial improvement, the elephant simply wasted away, getting progressively weaker and more atrophied.

The crush was 14.3 feet long and six feet wide.[6] Made with five-inch pipe, there were four side rails with fourteen inches between the lowest and second, twenty inches between the second and third, and 21 inches between the last two. The belly bar was equipped with an apparatus that could be moved forward and backward along a partial length of the crush. A cross brace was over the elephant with 27-inch diagonal beams supporting the top bars. Dr. Hartgrove constructed the ventral sled with four-inch pipe and was 72 inches wide by 18.5 inches deep. As the video displays, the rehabilitative crush was just a little bit bigger than Stoney and was meant to be used for a maximum of six months. Stoney, in contrast, was almost ten feet tall and weighed around seven thousand pounds. Stoney seemed pretty average in length, and if so he measured between eighteen and twenty-one feet long.[7]

The video depicts Mike putting Stoney through some brief commands such as "rise" and "move up." There is also a dog that periodically barks at the elephant. Advocates report this dog usually accompanied LaTorres during his visits with Stoney. Perhaps they were friends, a reminder of the long-ago Border Collie Travis. LaTorres has Stoney move his belly bar forward and backward approximately six feet and then tells the cameraperson, "See, he can move." Stoney repeatedly rises to his feet and settles back down onto the belly bar with loud chirps and squeaks. Dr. Hartgrove reported Stoney would loudly squeak thus when LaTorres would enter the barn to visit with him. Derby speculates that these vocalizations could be expressions of the endearment Stoney had for his trainer. After all, he was the only family Stoney had for most of the past decade. Knowing how social elephants are, one can assume his trainer was important to the elephant. As another vet of Stoney's would eventually say, one simply cannot stick an elephant away in a dark room mostly alone and expect him to heal.[8]

December arrived with bright sky and hope. There was optimism early in Stoney's isolation, as he was beginning to show signs of learning to walk on three legs. Mostly, though, it appears the months proceeded without proper physical therapy. After the first hopeful week of December, winter turned dark. Devastatingly, Stoney suffered another injury on December 12, 1994. During a physical therapy session, Stoney fell and injured his other rear leg as well as re-injuring his left one. This was likely a turning point in Stoney's life. Until this new injury, Dr. Hartgrove was optimistic regarding the elephant's eventual recovery. However, this development made the case more complex, and it made the prescribed physical therapy much more important. Later there was more brief hope that Stoney might be able to walk on three legs. After all, elephants have learned to walk while missing a leg before, as portrayed in Don Tayloe's documentary *The Last Elephants in Thailand*. The film shows elephants at a Thai elephant hospital that have stepped on land mines near the Burmese border learning to walk on three legs. Everyone hoped that Stoney might be able to do the same even if he could not completely heal from his injury. If he could three-leg ambulate, he could be retired and live some kind of life. Ultimately, the video depicts a Stoney with feces-covered rear legs moving awkwardly forward and backward five or six feet at a time in between rest periods on the clearly unpadded belly bar. Four separate veterinarians stressed the need for this padding and therapy in no uncertain terms, including Dr. Wendy Koch of the USDA and Dr. Martin Dinnes, as well as Drs. Schmidt and Hartgrove.

Until the December re-injury, there was much hope for Stoney's recovery. Hartgrove writes:

> We have maintained Stoney in a crush…treated him with oral Ibuprophen and topical DMSO [a painkiller]. Complications

from maintenance in the crush have been limited to pressure sores, which have been treated with topical DMSO/Betadine or Silvadene cream, and some sloughing of the foot pad which has been treated by trimming and Koppertox...Stoney was making excellent progress and was bearing some weight [on the injured leg]. Then in December he somehow reinjured his leg. He has made slower progress since then...he bears only minimal weight on it in the extended position. The original time for maintenance in the crush was predicted to be about six months. However with re-injury it becomes longer...as time goes on the prognosis for complete recovery becomes less optimistic. The question is will Stoney, given more time in the crush, begin to bear more weight and adapt to this injury or will this injury lead to his demise?

The month and year ended. The year 1995 dawned with decreased optimism for Stoney due to the recent re-injury. As the months dragged on, this cycle of well-intentioned and concerned vets requesting things for Stoney and Stoney's not always getting them continued. This puzzled the vets and USDA inspectors, and in the meantime, word of this situation got out to the public, including some tireless animal activists closely connected to the relentless Linda Faso.

Chapter 8

Activism and Disgruntled Vets

Winter yielded to spring. It was not until April 1995, Stoney's seventh month in the crush, that animal activists such as Faso and Derby learned of his months-long confined recovery in a maintenance barn behind a Las Vegas casino. They acted immediately on his behalf, and public interest increased. Activists began calling and writing to the USDA-APHIS, the Luxor, and other individuals and organizations. Often, the early letters and phone calls apparently were ignored. Regardless of her insistence that her only concern was to help Stoney, Faso's inquiries were met with silence. She and others discovered four vets examined Stoney and that three of them advised that Stoney's injury was permanent. Another new development they uncovered was that LaTorres had decided to retire Stoney and put a plan in place to move him to an elephant facility in Arkansas. Before his journey could begin, however, Stoney had to attain a certain level of health and mobility in order to make the move safely.

The minutes of the Luxor staff meeting dated March 21, 1995[1] read, "Luxor Elephant still on property due to an injury of torn ligament, now reported to be recovering nicely." It is very probable this is exactly what management believed and that there was no willful misrepresentation on the hotel's part. Truthfully, however, Stoney was not recovering nicely. Two months later, on May 24, 1995, a television reporter read a ten-second spot: "'Winds of the Gods' elephant Stoney is on temporary leave. The fifteen-year-old Asian elephant injured his leg during rehearsals. He has dislocated his leg and a full recovery is expected." It is not surprising that Stoney's situation undulated in and out of the local media with various degrees of accuracy. For example, his age being reported at the time of his accident, fifteen, is incorrect. These incomplete media snippets were common. They begin appearing directly after his injury. Back on September 24, 1994, KLAS Las Vegas local channel 8 ran a brief report on the injury at 6:30 pm local time also saying that Stoney injured his leg and was expected to make a complete recovery.

PAWS and other activists wanted to discover the entire story and tell it to the public. They believed that the humans who insist on having animals entertain them should likewise insist on their proper treatment when things go wrong. They thought this was not the case with Stoney. The local public who would like to have seen him perform, for the most part, did not join the activists on the street. PAWS became aware of the situation in April of 1995, and as the weeks passed, due to the expansive network of activism rather than the corridors of mainstream media—which soon moved on to other stories—Stoney's story spread like proverbial wildfire. Even the national news program *20/20* expressed some interest, though it didn't follow up for unknown reasons. The casino reminded activists that the Luxor never owned Stoney; LaTorres retained full control of and responsibility for the elephant. Not mollified, Faso and other activists began filing requests under the Freedom of Information Act in April to fill in their knowledge gaps.

Derby sought to understand the severity of his injuries and to improve his situation. Requests to meet with hotel executives and LaTorres were denied, and PAWS was assured that the situation was under control. An appeal to the USDA-APHIS was PAWS' next step, but the agency took no action. PAWS even offered to take Stoney to their elephant sanctuary and relocate and rehabilitate him entirely at their expense to no avail. PAWS and others began discovering details to add to their information dissemination campaign.

Early summer brought tourists and information. The requested Freedom of Information Act (FOIA) requests began to arrive and confirm some rumors and dispel others. In June, the USDA-APHIS found Stoney's means of primary conveyance, his trailer, still was not equipped with proper support structure, neither was the temperature inside the trailer maintained "at a level to ensure animals' healthful and comfortable transport."[2] With 95F degrees inside the trailer, ventilation was also inappropriate. There were only four small holes serving as vent openings. Two were on the front wall and two on the rear door, each of them only three inches in diameter. Of course, Stoney was not currently using this trailer, but it provides information because this is the same unheated and uncooled trailer Stoney traveled in during the majority of his life across the United States and into Canada. And if he were to be moved to the Arkansas facility, this might be the trailer in which he would again travel.

The inspector also wanted veterinary updates from the new attending vet plus a written protocol describing how LaTorres would handle Stoney during the transfer. The report also found the hygiene of Stoney's enclosure and crush problematic, observing "the animal is confined in a restricted enclosure (per attending vet) and rear feet stand in an area contaminated by a large pile of feces." This comment was common on many of the vet and USDA-APHIS inspection reports. Finally, the inspector ordered that LaTorres notify animal care inspection services at least forty-eight hours prior to Stoney's transport to Arkansas in order to "facilitate inspection of transport facilities and handling" due to "the nature of the animal's injury and requirements for special handling." Some doubted that Stoney could survive the cross-country relocation after being isolated in the crush for nearly nine months and receiving little to (possibly) no physical therapy or socialization during that time. There were even concerns regarding how he may react to sunlight after being indoors for so long.

Summer gained ground. June, July, and early August passed with similar activity and Stoney standing in his crush. Further complicating matters for activists, the facility that agreed to take Stoney endured its own allegations. Advocates claimed that bullhooks, electric prods, and other means of controlling elephants had been employed at the facility. As mentioned earlier, some elephant authorities endorse these tools. However, PAWS and the Tennessee Elephant Sanctuary both condemn these techniques, as do many others, including global elephant authorities Drs. Joyce Poole and Cynthia Moss, The Detroit Zoo, and the Oakland Zoo. PAWS cofounder Ed Stewart, an elephant expert in his own right with over thirty years of experience working with elephants and other exotic animals, reiterates his belief that no reputable elephant sanctuary would use bull-hooks or electric prods. Derby submitted a written request to the USDA that they closely oversee Stoney's transportation and carefully monitor him on a regular basis at his new location. She stated concern since she knew three bull elephants had died at the facility within a short time.[3]

PAWS wrote to the Deputy Administrator of USDA-APHIS on August 25, 1995: "PAWS is totally opposed to the planned movement of Stoney the elephant from the Luxor Hotel in Las Vegas to an elephant breeding farm in Arkansas." They asked the USDA to confiscate Stoney immediately and remove him to a facility where they believed he would receive proper veterinary care. Despite several veterinarians' and others' best efforts, it appears Stoney may well have been suffering. No visits from Travis, no walks in the woods, no playing in forest creeks and ponds. No night sleeping in the company of Sally unless those are the things he remembered during those dark, isolated months.

Late summer arrived. Another PAWS letter written in August

addressed to a top executive in Circus Circus Enterprises (also referred to as "CCE" hereafter) expresses similar concerns. While very clearly not assigning blame to CCE, the letter offers to fly in a vet at PAWS' expense to examine Stoney and provide a prognosis for his future. Also, if Stoney was found to be able to travel, Derby and other advocates again suggested that Stoney should go to the teaching veterinary hospital at the University of California at Davis. Finally, PAWS once again offered to accept Stoney into their sanctuary near Sacramento where they were already constructing both a ten-foot-deep physical therapy pool for two other elephants they were treating and an approximately one-acre enclosure complete with a climate-controlled barn with a built-in squeeze for medical treatment. Derby had been attempting to contact officials since May to no avail, and no one answered this letter either. It is known, however, that an agreement had already been reached with the Arkansas facility, and Circus Circus Enterprises spent a great deal of money constructing a new elephant barn in Arkansas and a duplicate of Stoney's cattle crush inside a transport truck.

More USDA-APHIS reports unearthed through FOIA requests document more discoveries from earlier that month. One dated August 3, 1995, states Stoney's medical log notes were not up to date. The latest vet entry is dated July 5. The inspector from June 19 required new attending vet evaluations to be submitted. As of this report, they had not been. Again, it appears LaTorres had ignored USDA-APHIS' orders, yet no penalty was levied against him or any other organization responsible for Stoney's welfare. The inspector writes, "There is no information in the animal medical log to indicate daily physical therapy sessions." Also, the report notes animal waste had been placed in a wheel-barrow, uncovered, inside the enclosure about ten feet from the elephant. Near the wheelbarrow, the inspector observed a "slight buildup of flies near the rear of the animal's crush." Relatedly, a considerable buildup of "feces odor" permeated the barn and was noticeable from outside. There were ventilation concerns, and the inspector ordered LaTorres to correct all this by the following day.

The last veterinary inspection of the crush's metal ventral support bar (still unpadded in late August) was on April 5, some four months prior. The first request for padding was nine months previous, in November, 1994. The new attending vet (the much respected Dr. Martin Dinnes had replaced Thomas Hartgrove as Stoney's official vet on May 22, 1995. He remained Stoney's attending vet until the end.

The plan to transport Stoney to Arkansas was now well underway. The trailer had been modified for increased ventilation, though it was not completely prepared for transport. The outside temperature was 105F, and temperature inside the trailer was 88F. The casino ordered protective grills to be in place on the side vent doors prior to transport, and again LaTorres was required to contact the inspection service at least forty-eight hours prior to transport. The same report denotes a further dietary concern: "the animal's current diet consists of grass, hay, and grain. Animal is not currently receiving any fresh produce or other supplements due to lack of refrigeration. Attending vet has not endorsed this as an appropriate diet. Correct by 8-4-95." LaTorres added additional hay to his diet as well as other foods. Upon receipt of this report through a FOIA request, activists again offered to provide the needed produce and a refrigerator at their own expense to the elephant barn. Faso says the request was ignored.

PAWS understands that it seems clear Stoney's care was the responsibility of his owner and not the Luxor or anyone else. It also seems his trainer didn't properly feed him, didn't always provide physical therapy, or provide permanent padding for his crush. Regardless, it was clearly still the USDA with which PAWS took the most issue. They primarily blamed the governmental entity responsible for the oversight of endangered species such as

Stoney, not Stoney's trainer and lifelong companion. By early August, activist interest was raging. Protests outside the Luxor increased, and PAWS kept people outside Stoney's barn documenting comings and goings around the clock. The local media were running stories, and an increasing amount of people were beginning to learn that an elephant had been kept immobile in a warehouse for the better part of a year. Public interest reached an all-time high by mid-August.

PAWS' activists report they observed LaTorres to visit Stoney only twice daily until the casino hired him to stay there and care for him full time in August. Speaking to this, an August letter from Dr. Martin Dinnes says LaTorres had to take employment that kept him away from the elephant "10–12 hours a day." He also reports, "Once this was discovered CCE advised Mr. LaTorres to quit his job and paid for him to stay and care for Stoney." PAWS reports LaTorres was away from the elephant up to twenty hours a day, but even if Dinnes' version is accepted as truth, an immobile elephant should not be left isolated for up to twelve hours daily. It appears the hotel agreed since they hired LaTorres to stay with Stoney full time. They were trying to help.

It is very expensive to maintain an elephant properly, and history is rife with cases of performing elephants (such as the upcoming story of Big Mary) being cast away due to injury or other causes that rendered them no longer profitable. Some elephants used in performance have suffered due to a sudden drop in their profitability or because they suddenly became a liability. As August wore on outside his metal building, Stoney languished in his crush.

Of note, one PAWS newsletter remarked that Stoney was being kept in a "torture device" during his isolation, and this deeply offended Dr. Hartgrove. He believed the comment failed to take into consideration the true intended rehabilitative nature of the apparatus and was a purely emotional and uninformed attack. This statement regarding the device alienated Tom

Hartgrove from the advocacy groups trying to help Stoney. He felt attacked for trying to help Stoney. This is an unfortunate aspect of this story. In a statement to USDA-APHIS investigator Greg Wallen, Dr. Michael Schmidt counters PAWS' negative assessment of the rehab device, praising the crush constructed for Stoney by Hartgrove:

> I had numerous telephone conversations with Dr. Hartgrove on the treatment of the acute rear leg injury to this elephant. What was done for the elephant, i.e. the creation of a special chute and resting platform, was both innovative and effective in giving this elephant a chance to heal the leg.

To travel back in time for a moment, Dr. Hartgrove installed the crush, replacing the original makeshift sling on October 1, 1994, just eight days after his injury. Dr. Hartgrove truly wanted to help Stoney and worked closely with him from September 25, 1994, until May, 1995. In early April, it appeared things were getting a little better for Stoney under his watch. In a report dated near the end of his tenure as Stoney's attending vet, Hartgrove's notes suggest some improvement. He writes:

> Stoney has dropped some weight since we first put him in the crush. However, this was desired to help decrease stress on injured leg. He weight bears minimally when the leg is extended, but will bear weight on knee and foot in flexed position. He is bright, alert, and eating. The pressure sores have improved and are static at this point.

His observations seem positive. At this point, he recommended to "continue to maintain him in the crush. Continue to remove sled (ventral support) for physical therapy sessions daily. In addition we will attempt to remove him from the crush to test his ability to ambulate and hopefully build muscle and strength for weight bearing." Drs. Hartgrove and Dinnes believed that if their directions were followed positive outcomes were possible. After the re-injury in December, Stoney had made progress in the preceding eight months.

Moving forward to spring, 1995, Dr. Schmidt writes that back in March "the Luxor casino wanted an opinion on whether the elephant could be moved. My examination of the elephant revealed that he was in great shape mentally, but that the leg had not healed." He wrote that the elephant was not ready to be moved and that he made some suggestions "to Dr. Hartgrove, whom I assumed would maintain his role as attending veterinarian." All of the vets had their own practices and lives and could not be on the premises daily. It was up to the trainer (who of course had his own life to attend to as well) to carry out their instructions, and Dr. Schmidt added his opinion that "with hindsight, I believe I can conclude that there should have been regular supervision by an attending veterinarian and resources supplied so that daily care was done in a thorough and assiduous manner." It seems LaTorres may have needed more help. Hardly anyone could be expected to see to this great responsibility on one's own. Perhaps it is unfortunate that the offers of help from PAWS were not taken advantage of.

Additionally, the owner, hotel, and advocacy group could have worked in concert for the best outcome regarding Stoney. Hopefully in the future, similar parties will have better coordination. Many animal advocates are not categorically opposed to all zoos, and regarding many zoos, the converse is true in relation to animal advocacy organizations. Regarding this theory of mutual cooperation, a praxis is emerging in the animal advocacy world. Though the few zealots get all the press, many might be surprised by the flexibility and reasonableness of contemporary animal advocates. It may even be likened to an emerging new wave of animal advocacy standing in stark contrast to the media representations of animal rights activists, but that is beyond the purview of this book.

Dr. Hartgrove left the case and reports that Stoney's situation had a tremendous impact on his view of animal welfare and his perception of other aspects of advocacy he had not previously seriously considered. He says he was not prepared for what would happen to Stoney, how the case and his death would eventually play out. He states:

> Stoney's life and death was a very challenging, frustrating and emotionally charged experience for me. The minute I met him I realized that I was faced with a task that I had not been trained for. It also quickly became apparent to me that I lacked a professional network capable of supporting me, both scientifically and emotionally. Certainly it was a world that I had never traveled in before.[4]

Dr. Hartgrove believed he lacked support. Hartgrove is a professional who has pledged to help save and improve animal lives, but he was not prepared for all of the colorations of Stoney's case.

However, Dr. Hartgrove was never satisfied that LaTorres was following his prescribed instructions properly. This dissatisfaction is well documented in public record by both Dr. Hartgrove and Dr. Dinnes. In an affidavit sworn by Thomas Hartgrove dated September 7, 1995, he reports:

> Mr. LaTorres did not follow my instructions to the letter. For example, we, Dr. Schmidt [the previously mentioned Dr. Mike Schmidt from Washington Park Zoo] and I wanted him to pad the crush and he did not do this. Sometimes I would show up at the facility and would find the elephant standing in manure. Since Mr. LaTorres did not follow the letter of my instructions I don't think it affected the outcome of Stoney.

Stoney's last attending vet, Dr. Martin Dinnes (also one of the vets for the Siegfried and Roy famous tiger show), had similar concerns. He changed the animal's diet, medication regime, and husbandry practices he believed were inadequate upon assuming the role of veterinarian of record for Stoney. He instructed LaTorres to teach Stoney how to walk on three legs, to move him back and forth within the crush, and eventually to move out of the stanchion and back into it. He writes, "The animal showed some improvement over the past 3-4 months prior to his death on August 28, 1995."

Dr. Dinnes wrote a letter on September 13th, 1995, which lends further context regarding the weeks leading up to his demise. It is addressed to Mr. J. David Neal, a senior investigator with USDA-APHIS. On September 12, Senior Investigator Neal called Dr. Dinnes with questions regarding LaTorres and Stoney. Dinnes says he was not involved when the injury occurred and references the involvement of Portland Zoo's Dr. Michael Schmidt and Dr. Thomas Hartgrove. The letter demonstrates very clearly that Dr. Dinnes had an experience similar to Dr. Hartgrove's and was not satisfied with LaTorres' actions regarding the elephant. Neal asked Dinnes where the trainer erred with respect to Stoney. The vet didn't seem to know what to make of Mike. Dinnes writes that "Mr. LaTorres [was] a nice person, he seemed honest, and he was not guilty of physically or mentally abusing the animal. Where I have (or had) a problem with Mr. LaTorres was with his apparent nonchalant or non-caring attitude toward the animal." Regarding LaTorres' caring for Stoney, Dinnes writes. "I feel that he did not provide the animal with the level of animal husbandry practices consistent with those required to properly care for an elephant." The letter goes on to clearly state that Dr. Dinnes experienced considerable frustration with Mike's approach to Stoney's care.

For most who hear Stoney's story, it remains difficult to understand why the dietary concerns were not addressed and why the belly bar remained unpadded for the highly endangered elephant. Numerous vet and inspection reports cite pressure sores from rubbing against it for months on end. Stoney had a sore on his head he had rubbed raw from grating against the upper portion of the crush. This too needed padding and lacked it. Specifically regarding the lack of padding on the crush, Dinnes writes, "I can attest to the fact that my instructions to provide padding on the ventral body support that the animal leaned on were not followed. I was told 'tomorrow, tomorrow' or 'I padded it but it doesn't last except for a few days.'" Dinnes continues, "I can vouch that, as pointed out by others who visited the animal and Mr. LaTorres in my company, all asked me 'what the guy's problem was' with respect to his attitude toward the animal.'"[5]

Dinnes also writes about the amount of time LaTorres spent with Stoney while he was immobilized in the crush. The veterinarian writes that LaTorres took necessary employment that kept him away from Stoney for "10–12 hours a day." Regarding this he reports that:

> Once this was discovered, CCE advised Mr. LaTorres to quit his job and paid him to stay and care for Stoney. Mr. LaTorres should have known that you can't leave an elephant by itself, uncared for, for 10-12 hours a day—even a healthy elephant!

Dinnes goes on to write, "I suspect that while I was not the attending veterinarian, that Mr. LaTorres was not routinely administering the prescribed medication to Stoney. I mentally monitored his supplies from time to time." All four vets who examined Stoney questioned the care and diet Stoney received.

Dinnes concludes his letter with a statement reminding Senior Investigator Neal that it was Mike LaTorres, not he or CCE, who owned the elephant. Therefore, neither he nor CCE had any power to remove the elephant from LaTorres' care. He also notes LaTorres was the only person who could handle the elephant and that he did so very skillfully. Dinnes concludes, "In sum, I could not comprehend, during the time of my exposure to and involvement with Mr. LaTorres, his attitude, level of concern, truthfulness, his overall care of the animal or his lack of proper judgment."

Neither Mike nor Stoney walk this earth any longer. LaTorres—who remained publically silent until the very end—followed Stoney to the grave in just a few short years. Tracking Mike and Stoney through their years together provides a widely incomplete picture of the actual man who was Stoney's owner and handler. USDA-APHIS reports, vet records, court records, security reports, safety inspections, health certificates, brief video footage, and interviews with Sally LaTorres and people only vaguely or tangentially associated with him were the only things that yielded any elucidation. No other ex-wives or family members could be reached except one who declined to participate. Nonetheless, I will attempt to speak on his behalf with the following statement: As LaTorres is now deceased, he should be given the benefit of the doubt. By many accounts, it appears Mike LaTorres was very nice and likeable. The reasons behind what he did or did not do regarding Stoney are unknown. None of us were there. Regardless of our intentions and convictions, we do not know that if faced with the same overwhelming situation we would have done anything differently. Action is contingent on numerous variables. Information on the man is sparse. Nevertheless, a good deal of information is available regarding the time leading up to Stoney the elephant's final day on Earth.

Chapter 9

The Death of Stoney

As of early July, the proposed relocation plan was in full swing. Dr. Dinnes made the decision that the elephant would have to be moved to the Arkansas elephant facility and provides details.[1] He also writes that CCE assumed all food and medical care responsibility for Stoney. The company provided $34,000 to build a suitable elephant barn on the Arkansas property to house Stoney. In addition, CCE sent LaTorres back to school in order to renew his expired commercial driver's license as well as renewing the license on his trailer and the appropriate insurance. At Dinnes' direction, CCE built a replica of the crush inside the trailer and further modified the ventilation system. All in all, Circus Circus Enterprises generously spent nearly $100,000 in preparation for the planned move to Arkansas and things were looking up. However, Derby and other activists believed Stoney was in no condition to be moved and feared he might even die en route. The attitude of PAWS and other activists was that action must occur. As of early August, 1995, Stoney's condition was dire. According to vet reports, it appears he was suffering, and his physical problems were ever-mounting.

Dinnes wrote a letter to Dr. Koch outlining the plan for Stoney's safe transport.[2] After identifying himself as the newly appointed attending veterinarian by Circus Circus Enterprises with the approval of Stoney's trainer, he writes of the USDA's involvement in the transport of Stoney from the Luxor to Arkansas and addresses various welfare concerns. He reports on the initial injury. Dinnes describes Stoney as non-weight bearing on the injured leg and such condition has now resulted in "severe atrophy of all the muscles of his rear left leg." Dinnes describes the crush and notes more recent medical concerns such as the fact he has "sustained multiple decubital ulcers and deterioration of the foot pads and toes of all four feet." Decubital ulcers are sores due to arterial occlusion or prolonged pressure on a particular part of the body. The footpad deterioration problem was new and very serious. LaTorres remarked that Stoney's foot problems were a result of the great difficulty he had in providing proper foot care in his current condition.

The subject of elephants' feet is important. In captive elephants, good foot health is very difficult to maintain for a number of reasons. An expert in elephant foot problems, Murray E. Fowler, writes that foot problems are the single most important physical ailment of captive elephants.[3] Caring for elephants' feet is the most commonly performed task by elephant caretakers behind feeding and cleaning. Elephants' feet are designed to walk on spongy earth and uneven surfaces with some give. The majority of captive elephants spend the vast majority of their time standing on hard surfaces (most often concrete in zoos). Often they are standing in collections of feces and urine since many of them spend the nights inside barns. Dr. Elliot Katz says having elephants stand in dirty conditions on hard concrete floors is the single biggest problem with zoo captivity.[4] Grooms routinely trim away necrotic foot tissue until no foot pad at all remains. If an elephant cannot stand, he or she will die. The seriousness of foot problems cannot be underestimated.

It is so serious that, in 1998, the first American elephant foot care conference was held in Oregon. This First North American Conference on Elephant Foot Care and Pathology drew professionals from twenty-three states, Canada, India, and New Zealand and included professionals from over forty zoos, circuses, elephant sanctuaries, universities, and US colleges of veterinary medicine. It led to the publication of the book, *The Elephant's Foot: Prevention and Care of Foot Conditions in Captive Asian and African Elephants*. Fifty percent of captive elephants develop foot problems, with many resulting in death or serious disability. Some experts have suggested, "nonresolvable foot infection and arthritis are the major reasons for euthanizing elephants."[5] African, Asian, and African Forest elephant species all can have foot problems. Free-ranging elephants in their indigenous habitats also have some foot problems mainly from injuries, fractures, and embedding of foreign objects, but the preponderance of conditions such as foot rot occurs in captive elephants. The one exception is elephants forced to work in Indian and Southeast Asian work camps. The collective authors of the volume believe foot problems are the main physical problem with elephants in captivity.

If properly cared for and maintained on a spongy floor, such as the dirt floors of the barns at PAWS' elephant sanctuary as one example, many elephants in captivity do not develop foot problems. Elephants must move around and use their feet on various surfaces and not be confined near their waste. As of the August 17 letter, Stoney had been largely immobile for one week shy of eleven months, and USDA-APHIS' inspection reports clearly demonstrate he was often standing in feces and urine on a hard floor. It is not surprising that all four of his feet were experiencing problems and his hind right foot was rotting. Foot problem prevention is far preferable to any foot care treatment, and a nineteenth century elephant management manual demonstrates that this has been well known for a very long time. J.H. Steel's 1885 advice regarding elephant foot care could have alleviated some of Stoney's suffering:

> Diseases of the feet of the elephant are numerous and severe, and such as liable to absolutely incapacitate him for service. They are mostly due to want of care in his management and

are so preventable.[6]

Carol Buckley, cofounder of the Tennessee Elephant Sanctuary, contributes a chapter to *The Elephant's Foot*. She writes in reference to captive elephants and reiterates that lack of proper diet leads to elephant health problems. She writes that many factors contribute to the physical and psychological health of elephants, including diet, environment, and management: "when these factors are suboptimal, resulting in stress, the captive elephant's response will manifest in disorders of the mind and/or body."[7] To say the least, Stoney's environment was suboptimal, and his health steadily deteriorated as his isolation continued into late August, nearing a full year of isolation in the crush.

Buckley stresses that elephants need natural habitat for optimal foot health. Examining her definition of a natural habitat illustrates losses beyond foot care that Stoney endured. She writes a natural habitat must be:

> a vast space of diverse terrain and natural substrate, complete with wetlands, seeded and volunteer pastures, wooded areas, natural year-round water sources (including spring-fed ponds, washes, streams, and dry creek beds), and a wide range of live vegetation suitable for the species being maintained.[8]

Freedom of movement is essential. Buckley states "because an elephant in a natural–habitat environment is not confined to areas contaminated with waste and spends its day walking, eating, dusting, grazing, foraging, digging, bathing, and napping in a vast area, its psychological and physical needs are satisfied."[9] In natural habitats, trees provide nutrients and elements of foot-conditioning since elephants like to step, smash, and rub their feet on trees. They also use their feet like shovels to excavate soil after tearing away vegetation. Additionally, Buckley writes that their feet should almost always be moist. She says, "in the barn should be the only time their feet are not exposed to moisture."[10] Water cleans the footpad and keeps it lubricated. She continues, "When an elephant's foot is depleted of moisture by unnatural surfaces, such as concrete, the pad becomes dry and brittle and problems can develop." Moisture also acts as a conditioner, "softening dry areas [and keeping the pad] more supple."[11] Inside his shed, in the crush, Stoney was denied even the falling rain.

In a natural habitat or an acceptable protected contact habitat the elephant "is never chained. Free-choice access to the indoor facility enables the elephant to come and go at will."[12] With this free-choice access, captive elephants spend their time at activities of their choosing on natural substrate. Recalling Stoney's foot issues, Buckley writes, "chaining has many negative effects on foot health. Not only are elephants forced to stand in their own excrement, but they also rock and sway unnaturally...which can cause tissue damage as well as irregular wear and thin foot pads."[13] People often observe and remark upon side-to-side swaying and rocking in captive elephants, and it is never a normal behavior according to Buckley and Derby.

Most, if not all, of Buckley's suggestions for optimal foot health are also applicable to psychological health. It really is unknown if Stoney was suffering mentally, but his feet were rotting off. The conference's final recommendations apply to all elephants kept in captivity. The experts cite six recommendations:

1. Keeping elephants is expensive, and each institution should have proper resources.
2. A written exercise program for foot care should be kept.
3. Radiography should be performed at least annually on captive elephants.
4. Written foot care protocol should be maintained.

5. The amount of time elephants spend standing on hard surfaces should be minimal.
6. Thorough annual physical exams should be provided.

There is no record of these being provided for Stoney.

Dietary concerns continued. Dr. Dinnes examined the elephant on August 10, 1995, and wrote Stoney was on a grass, hay, bread, and limited produce diet of poor quality. Dr. Dinnes cites the aforementioned lack of refrigeration and lack of proper produce. At this point, CCE provided a refrigerator. Dinnes ordered a special higher-quality diet and CCE paid for this as well. In his reports, Dinnes continues to discuss diet and health recommendations he made to the trainer. He writes of Stoney, "I believe he was dehydrated prior to Wednesday August 9 based upon the amount of time Mr. LaTorres was able to devote to tending the animal." He continues, "Mr. LaTorres, of necessity, had undertaken other employment." As noted, eventually CCE asked him to quit his job and stay at the shed to tend to the elephant full time. For so doing, CCE paid him an equivalent income to the job he quit. This agreement was reached on or around August 9, 1995. Finally, Stoney would have more time with his trainer and vice versa. Perhaps LaTorres would now have a little more financial support. He was still the owner and the sole person responsible for Stoney, but CCE's new arrangement must have alleviated some of his stress.

More medical conditions and suggestions are noted in the August 17 letter as Stoney's condition had worsened. Dinnes' veterinary notes read:

The animal is grossly underweight due to the diet...he was on and because of the severe muscle atrophy of all muscles of his left leg and on the left side of his upper back. There is some atrophy anteriorly on the left side of his back as well...the loss of weight due to muscle atrophy is permanent...The animal's feet are not in good condition...there's a good possibility that he will lose (and replace) his entire right rear foot pad.

The vet's August 17 letter continues to state that the elephant was unstable from the standpoint of his debilitated condition, but "also in the areas of pain and discomfort. I'm very concerned about these factors as well as the future health of his entire right rear leg and its joints." In short, there were problems with his originally uninjured rear leg as well. Progress from the December re-injury was not outstanding. Elephants have adapted to walk on three legs, but an elephant with both rear legs rendered unusable has no hope at all. Dinnes writes that Stoney must remain in the crush until he and LaTorres could teach him to stand and walk on three legs.

It seems the vet hoped that Stoney could be transferred to Arkansas and there have a better chance at recovery. Critics of the move, again, believed he wasn't yet strong enough. Derby and Stewart again suggested he be taken to a much closer teaching veterinary hospital at the University of California at Davis to receive better quality veterinary care. It is unclear if this suggestion was considered, as no one commented on it in the public record. In conclusion, Dinnes reported to the USDA's Dr. Koch that "the prognosis for this animal is extremely poor." Attempted x-rays of Stoney's rear legs were unsuccessful, and the vet put him on non-steroidal anti-inflammatory medication, pain relief, and Chondroitin Sulfate in hopes of preserving his other healthy joints.

On a positive note, due to the refrigerator now present, one local elderly woman named Carol Arnow asked Mike if she could bring Stoney some fresh fruit from time to time. Mike agreed and allowed her to visit him a few times a week. Carol later spoke very highly of Mike. She considered him and Stoney her friends until the day she died.

Fruit aside, the planned relocation gets more detailed from

this point in the August 17 letter. Stoney was to be transported to Arkansas via a well-ventilated tractor-trailer with a replica of the crush built inside it. The trip should take two to three days. Protocol for movement from the barn to the transport truck is also provided. This was thought to be the most difficult part of the operation due to Stoney's atrophy and injuries. Under this protocol section, it is noted that Stoney was being taught to ambulate on three legs with the damaged one bearing some weight. Stoney had progressed in this activity to the point he could now "be totally backed out of the existing stanchion and then return to it moving in a forward direction." Stoney would not have to negotiate any steps or ramps. He would be able to move "from the barn to the trailer along one, level plane of hard packed dirt" that would be constructed. Emergency measures would include a crane "equipped with various belting and pipe supports" in case the animal "goes down and requires assistance in getting back on his feet." The crane operator had experience helping Dinnes in similar situations. Also, the plan was that "the loading will be done at night because of ambient temperature factors and security reasons." Once loaded, Stoney's crush was to be disassembled, transported, and "reassembled in the animal's new barn which Circus Circus Enterprises has built, at their own expense, at Riddle's Elephant Sanctuary in Arkansas."

Such was the plan, but Dr. Koch of the USDA-APHIS did not immediately approve. She wrote a detailed letter in reply requesting more information regarding the recovery regimen and the transport plan. She writes to Dr. Dinnes, "your letter does not address your recommendations concerning the 'training' or 'physical therapy' which should be given to Stoney to allow him to begin moving around under his own power." She requested therapy information such as "what type of action for what periods of time" because the USDA-APHIS "would like to follow up on this aspect of his treatment as well." She needed more detail on the transport plan because the USDA-APHIS was "particularly concerned about this transport because the elephant's condition will make any trip extremely stressful for him." She then asks for elucidation on several points. Her many questions request much more detail and include the following inquiries:

> Who will be involved in the actual transport...will there be an attendant or only a driver? What is the experience of the people involved? What is the route of travel and the planned stops? How long will each rest period be? How often will the animal be fed and watered? Will food and water be carried or obtained along the way? If carried, how will it be stored? If procured, how will it be obtained? How often will the trailer be cleaned during the transport? What are the plans to ensure that adequate emergency veterinary care is available if necessary? What are the plans to handle other possible emergencies such as a breakdown in an isolated area on a hot and humid day? What are the plans for unloading the animal at the destination? Will a veterinarian be present to ensure that any negative impact of the trip on the animal's condition is cared for in a timely manner? Regulations require that the animal be checked at least every four hours while traveling. Documentation of such checks...should be maintained...the temperature should not be allowed outside the range of 45–85 degrees Fahrenheit...what are the plans if the acceptable temperature range is breached?

The USDA-APHIS seeks to document activities such as this proposed move. In this case, the agency was concerned that everyone involved should provide the best experience for Stoney's move. Koch writes she would like to be "assured that an extremely lame elephant will be transported in a way commensurate with its optimal well-being" and invites Dinnes and LaTorres to provide those assurances. She concludes, "The actual transportation of this elephant should not take place until we have received your response to this letter and approved your proposals for ensuring the animal's welfare during the transport." She also states the USDA-APHIS must be supplied with the exact time of the transport so they "can arrange to have an inspector present during the loading process."

Koch has a reputation as an excellent vet and animal care specialist who truly cares for the many animals with whom she works. If the USDA-APHIS is to be criticized for not leveling penalties after repeated failed inspections and the like, it is not Dr. Koch who should bear that criticism. During research for this book, several sources reported highly of her. The fact that there was so much information required regarding his move is critical. It seems the health concerns were primary. If Stoney could not survive the actual move, activists asked, what did it matter which location was chosen? Regardless, a veterinary professional believed he could. The vet responded to Dr. Koch's letter, submitted proper paperwork and plans, and with the USDA-APHIS satisfied, the parties scheduled the move for August 28, 1995.

Earlier, when it became clear that Stoney was going to be transferred to the new facility, the protests became more heated, more desperate. The activists raged. Of them, Derby and Faso worked the hardest and the most diligently to try to help Stoney. Letter writing campaigns to the USDA-APHIS and other pertinent organizations were ineffective. Media appearances, public protests, vigils, demonstrations in front of the Luxor, and massive campaigning did not seem to help very much either.

Some actions were taken. Backing up to July of 1995, Stoney's story hit the media in greater force than ever before, and the public became aware of Stoney. They were not pleased. The period of July and August was a key period for Stoney-focused activism.

Perhaps there was a somewhat unavoidable adversarial

feeling between activists such as Derby and entities such as LaTorres and the hotel. PAWS conducted the first advocacy activity. A press release dated July 10, 1995, announces "A vigil for Stoney the Forgotten Elephant at the Luxor Hotel." This took place on the corner of Hacienda and the Las Vegas Strip on the front sidewalk of the Luxor hotel that evening. The release summarizes his injury and his confinement on hotel property and references the Portland Zoo's elephant breeding program. It states, "Stoney is one of many bull elephants used up by a cruel and abusive industry, and discarded when no longer useful." The heated release discusses the rumor that he was to be moved to the Arkansas facility (not as of then verified) and opposes it on the grounds that he was not in good enough physical condition to breed, and farms such as it are not suited for crippled elephants. The demonstration occurred with good attendance, and the advocates demanded to know of Stoney's physical condition

By July Stoney was suffering from muscle atrophy and was standing in manure in addition to receiving an inadequate diet. Some activists attacked Mike LaTorres with angry and inaccurate words. Some advocates accused the hotel of keeping Stoney and his true medical condition secret due to fear of negative public relations and advocacy backlash. The hotel denied this. The hotel leadership may have been simply trying to focus on the problem or, quite possibly, may have been unaware of its seriousness. From an advocacy education standpoint, the demonstration was effective. The media were there.

The next day, July 11, the *Las Vegas Sun* ran an article, "Group Protests Fate of Injured Elephant." It mentions activists carrying signs. One reads, "Secrets of the Pyramid—Mysteries of the Hidden Elephant." A local activist holds a sign, "Can Stoney the Elephant Walk?" The writer quotes activist Loren Paglia in the article: "One day he's a star. He makes money for the casino. And then they dump him." Deservedly or not, the casino drew much heat from activists. The local activist push demanded they do something about it since Stoney was on Luxor property. *Las Vegas Sun* writer Bob Shemeligian wrote that Stoney "was one of the biggest stars—in more ways than one—of the 'Winds of the Gods' show at Luxor until [he] injured a hind leg practicing a stand." The situation heated up as more of the public demanded information and action. In a release, CCE Spokesperson Sarah Ralston emphatically said that the company was not "dumping" Stoney. She notes that Mike LaTorres owned Stoney, not Circus Circus. Ralston added, despite that fact, CCE "has spent $30,000 caring for the elephant in a specially built animal barn on the Luxor grounds." She said the corporation expected to spend another $10,000 to transport Stoney to a "breeding farm in Arkansas." In the end, and to their credit, they actually spent much more.

Advocates, including Faso, are quoted in the piece once again opposing the move to Arkansas. Faso says of the facility that "we understand that three other bull elephants died during some period and we question whether Stoney will survive there—if he survives the trip." Ralston responded by saying, "Riddle's breeding farm is an excellent retreat for Stoney. It's one of the few places in the country that takes elephants in need." The article mentions that negotiations in early spring broke down two months prior between CCE and PAWS. Then the article turns toward protestors' concerns that the animal had been kept in isolation since the accident in September of the previous year. Protestors are quoted: "I want to know what they have done with that elephant and why they have kept it so quiet," and "he's standing in his own feces...his feet can get infected." Faso states her strong opinion that she understands LaTorres owns the animal and the hotel has spent thousands caring for him, but "that's not the issue. He was injured rehearsing for 'Winds of the Gods,' and so that makes the hotel responsible. And also, the issue is that Stoney should go to a sanctuary." The company disagreed, and their position is documented in the public record in the form of a September 17, 1995, *Las Vegas Sun* article titled "Hotel was not responsible for the tragedy of Stoney." The Shemeligian piece echoes that activists were further concerned at the time of the move that the elephant facility was not AZA accredited or a member of TAOS (The Association of Sanctuaries).[14] As July of 1995 proceeded, more letter writing, action alerts, and press releases were generated. Even though it was unknown to Stoney, his condition mattered to more people than Mike. To many people, he mattered. Derby and Faso never actually saw him, but he mattered to them. The activism became a maelstrom, a firestorm. Some say they can hardly help but sympathize for the overwhelmed LaTorres who endured fierce public attacks of often illogical and uninformed rhetoric. Others such as animal advocate Karen Davis of United Poultry Concerns disagree and point out that he had agency and freedom of decision and used both incorrectly.

PAWS wrote to USDA official Dr. Ron De Haven on July 17, 1995, summarizing the situation and citing several Animal Welfare Act violations, including section 3.129 (Stoney eating moldy bread and deteriorating produce) and section 3.126 (insufficient drainage, lighting, and ventilation). The letter questions the logic of sending Stoney to the facility in Arkansas. Derby also requested a USDA inspector be present when Stoney was loaded for transportation. She then expresses frustration regarding the USDA and its alleged lack of action on some cases. She writes:

> It is outrageous that this elephant...protected by the Animal Welfare Act, has been allowed to languish in filth, eat garbage, and live in constant pain in a maintenance shack at a luxury hotel for eleven months while no protective enforcement action has been taken by the USDA...while LaTorres has been "cited" for numerous violations, he has not been fined, had his USDA permit revoked, or had this pitiful

animal confiscated...the laws are there yet they are seldom ever enforced. Why?

The USDA did not respond.

The protests and demonstrations continued through July and into August. Activists wrote letters to government officials, the hotel, and other people even tangentially involved. There was the fervent and frantic near panic atmosphere that accompanies campaigns to get individual animals out of peril when time is believed to be of the essence. Advocates often cannot understand why animals' wellbeing, comfort, and mental states are often ignored for, what seems to them to be, the simple sake of profit. Other than the profit derived from their performances, Derby consistently argues that there is little logic in fetishizing the elephant and reducing it to a performing creature devoid of natural behavior. Taking advantage of people's natural affinity for big animals, PAWS maintains that elephant performance has little purpose beyond the profit margin. And when it comes to the people who become advocates for animals such as Stoney or Jenny (another elephant in danger mentioned in Derby's July 17 letter), advocates often experience a near-hopeless panic that can easily become rage and evolve further into resolution and finally to apathy and inaction or even deep depression. It is known that Derby, Faso, and the others who were helping them work on Stoney's behalf felt despair in their knowledge of Stoney's suffering and their inability to help him. The public did get involved, but the resulting slew of letters and other inquiries went mostly ignored.

Stoney and his suffering are paramount to this story. By August of 1995, the elephant was devastated and in a horrible condition by any standards. Dr. Dinnes' comments regarding Stoney's physical condition in his August 17 letter reported Stoney's permanent underweight status due to muscle atrophy, the fact that his right foot was rotting (likely aggravated from often standing in feces and urine), the fact that he was unstable in the areas of pain and discomfort, and that his prognosis for this animal was extremely poor. Stoney had deteriorated rapidly in his crush at this point. By the beginning of August of 1995, he likely had numerous skin conditions, pressure sores on his legs, belly, and face, severe muscle atrophy, severe foot conditions, severe leg conditions, underweight status, and dehydration. Additionally, I offer as a result of my research that at this point LaTorres would have likely been overwhelmed and possibly even at a loss, as might have been the hotel. Some have been critical of the Luxor's handling of the situation. However, many people believed the Luxor did an admirable job and spoke highly of it and CCE. Sally LaTorres believes the Luxor really tried to help Stoney by providing supplies, vet care, and paying for the barn to be built in Arkansas. Dr. Schmidt agrees, saying, "I believe the casino was trying to do the right thing for the elephant," even though he believed the resources and personnel allocated to the project proved to be inadequate. The hotel reminded the activists and the public several times that Stoney's quarters were well-lit, climate controlled, and USDA approved. All true.

Often expressed is the belief that the government has licensing and overseeing agencies, such as the USDA-APHIS, to make sure that animals are protected as well as the Animal Welfare Act and laws to protect endangered species. While it is true USDA-APHIS does a good job of documenting certain animals, large problems exist that the agency cannot oversee. Primarily, they do not have unlimited funding; far from it. Even though exhibitors are inspected, it is truly up to the individual owners of performing animals to comply with the suggestions made for their animals' welfare. Stoney's case is a pertinent example of how the system can break down. According to Faso, the law currently requires only annual USDA inspections unless there are reported problems. In addition, very rarely are actual fines or penalties levied for USDA-APHIS violations. If matters get bad enough, lawsuits certainly ensue, as was the case with Stoney. However, the agency simply does not have enough work force to provide the proper amount of oversight. As with almost everything in American government, it comes down to funding, or rather the lack of it. Of course, if all trainers and owners would do the right thing and receive proper support, less oversight would be required. As of April, 2010, there was currently no animal care inspector at all in the state of Nevada.[15] Agents from other states come into Nevada for annual inspections and documentation. The lack of manpower and funding is significant.

Derby, Faso, and others kept writing letters until the very end and beyond. A blistering August 26 press release titled, "Secrets of the Luxor Pyramid—The Mystery of the Hidden Elephant," lists both of them as contacts. It announces "PAWS, a national animal organization with more than 10,000 members around the nation, (50,000 as of early 2013) will hold a press conference outside the Luxor hotel…to expose the terrible treatment and torture of an elephant named Stoney." The torture accusation enraged some of the involved entities, who felt constantly attacked and presented in an unfair light by PAWS and other activists. In the release, PAWS describes Stoney as having "been kept in total darkness hanging in a mechanical device… According to USDA reports, he is standing in his own urine and feces; he is covered with flies; and he has had no veterinary attention in four and a half months!" According to Derby, "If AWA [Animal Welfare Act] statutes were enforced by the USDA, there would be no elephants traveling in circuses and Stoney would not be hanging from a sling in the Luxor Hotel!" If Stoney were to be transferred to Arkansas, PAWS stated they would be following the truck the entire way to monitor his treatment and his condition. And the planned move was still very much in effect. PAWS and local activists vowed to be there until the very bitter end. They were. Despite their protests, the proposed relocation was going forward. Then came August 27.

The most verifiable version of the August 27 and 28 events comes from USDA-APHIS Animal Care Inspector Wallen who was present to monitor the loading and the moving of Stoney as promised in Koch's letter. He is known as a good person and a competent inspector. No longer with the USDA, Wallen's carefully written summary of events provide verifiable and valuable facts regarding the incident and certain events since Stoney arrived in Vegas on March 1, 1994, eighteen months before Wallen's observations. The report begins "This report summarizes the operations of the subject's Las Vegas site from February 1994 to August 1995."

The year is succinctly recapped in Wallen's report. He writes that in February of 1994 he was informed that Stoney and his trainer would be arriving for an extended engagement at the Luxor hotel and casino. He notes that LaTorres arrived on March 1 accompanied by a male Asian elephant named Stoney. They were housed in facilities provided by the hotel. Both the housing site and the performance site inside the hotel were properly inspected and were found to be in compliance. Stoney's housing site is described as "a warehouse on hotel property." This is the same building eventually outfitted with the crush. As mentioned earlier, the first violation occurred on March 2 involving the ageing transport trailer, Stoney's primary means of conveyance. During an interview on March 3, the trainer stated that they left the Florida site in late January, 1994. The report states Clark County Animal Control was notified of the presence of the elephant on March 3. Stoney had arrived.

The next date mentioned in the summary of events is September 23, 1994, the night Stoney initially tore his tendon and was transported many hours later to his barn by means of a hotel dumpster. The concise summary is of interest since it has been examined in such detail in previous chapters. It reads:

On September 23, 1994 the animal was involved in a mishap at the showroom, backstage, prior to an evening performance. For reasons unknown, the animal fell while doing a hind-leg stand and injured his left hind leg. The attending vet was contacted immediately. He supervised the animal's movement from the hotel back to the holding barn. The animal was examined, tests were conducted and treatments and medications were prescribed. The attending vet consulted with other veterinary experts who determined that the animal should be housed in a special support device for a recuperation of approximately six months."

Moving closer to August 27 and 28 1995, other things are noted. On December 21, 1994, the attending vet "reported all had been well until December 12, 1994, when the animal, after feeling better and acting stronger, re-injured his leg during a therapy session." It appears Stoney did receive some physical therapy when the vets were present, but at least two vets theorized that these may be some of the only times he did. Also in December, the report continues, the restricted housing and rehabilitation were ordered to be continued for "several more months." A fifth official, Dr. Ron DeHaven, visited in February to evaluate Stoney's housing and condition and made observations similar to those of other doctors.

In March of 1995, the inspector was informed that the elephant would likely be transferred to another facility and permanently retired. Over the next two months, the USDA sector office was contacted, paperwork was submitted, and a follow-up inspection on May 3, 1995, "reported numerous category III NCIs." Category III denotes first-time violations. Dinnes officially became Stoney's new attending vet on May 22, 1995, and in mid-June more category III violations occurred regarding the failure to submit new vet status reports and poor sanitation practices. The violations increased. Inspector Wallen reports that on August

3, 1995, he conducted a re-inspection and "cited the licensee for several category III direct NCI's and reported a violation for failure to provide appropriate veterinary care." Wallen was present for Dr. Dinnes' examination of Stoney on August 9. At this late point in the game, it is easily fair to say that Stoney was suffering, to some degree, every day despite the efforts of all involved.

After the back and forth of the letters between Drs. Dinnes and Koch, the proper paperwork was submitted and the relocation plan was set in motion. Greg Wallen was the USDA-APHIS representative to oversee the loading and transportation of Stoney. Dr. Dinnes contacted Inspector Wallen at 10.00 am on August 28, 1995, and told him of a problem. The day before, August 27, while Stoney was undergoing a therapy and exercise session, he fell and injured his right leg. The elephant had been down since then, and they could not get him back up. Wallen immediately reported the situation to De Haven and traveled to Stoney's barn. Wallen's supervisor clearly told him that the animal could not be transported unless he could stand and support himself under his own power.

When Stoney fell on August 27, his good leg (a relative term at this point with its footpad rotting off and its increasing muscular atrophy) was badly injured. Over the next twenty-four hours, Stoney struggled to stand and could not. Though they did not know what was happening, the activists outside could hear his screams and his struggles and a video camera was taping the outside of the building.

The footage is available for viewing via You Tube. At the time of publication, the video was available via YouTube at the following unwieldy link: http://www.youtube.com/watch?v=Sc5T5dNzMF8. PAWS released to the public in hopes of raising awareness. The video first shows thirty-one seconds of Stoney performing during a "Winds of the Gods" performance. Of interest is that during this clip Stoney performs hind-leg stands, the trick which led to his prolonged death. Following this, the clip shows him confined in his crush for approximately ninety seconds. This clarifies several things. First, it is apparent there are, in fact, no windows in his shed. Also, the ventral belly bar is clearly unpadded, there is waste behind his rear feet, and the black dog is also visible. Mike is heard giving Stoney a command to rise and is briefly seen. Actually seeing Stoney in his crush is a key factor into gaining understanding of his suffering, and all readers are encouraged to view it. For instance, after seeing Stoney in the crush it becomes apparent that he could not lie down during his eleven-month isolation. He had to sleep each night by leaning on the unpadded belly bar.

The last portion of the video shot on August 28 captured his screams during the attempts to get Stoney back on his feet. Though they can and do sleep lying down, if an elephant cannot rise to its feet after some time he or she will die, its massive weight crushing its internal organs.

This portion of the clip begins with a shot of the front of the barn with the garage type door rolled upward. August 28 is a blue-sky sunny day, and trees near the door partially obscure the view. The vantage point of the video is as close as advocates could get. A forklift drives into the barn while one of the filmers exclaims, "My God!" Power tools whir. At this point, Stoney had been down for nearly a day. These sounds and the forklift were attempts to get Stoney back on his feet. The plan to move Stoney to Arkansas was delayed at this point. Undoubtedly, the clear primary concern was to get Stoney back to his feet. He constantly struggled to rise and could not. At the video timestamp of 2:43, The viewer hears Stoney roaring in an intense vocalization. Seconds afterward, two men exit the barn and stand for a moment before returning to the shed. Other voices are heard inside, and a passerby wanders up and peers inside. The roar is powerful, more like a lion than an elephant.

Research has discovered what was occurring inside the

building near this time. Repeated attempts to upright Stoney failed. Eventually, after almost twenty-four hours of this, while workers were still trying to get him up, Stoney simply died. It is difficult and most important to understand that contrary to circulated reports, Stoney was not euthanized. He simply had more than he could physically withstand and possibly died of pain, exhaustion, or other fatal overload. Though he received painkillers, Stoney was not euthanized. He died on the feces-covered floor near his crush in the windowless quarters at the age of twenty-two.

The inspection report of Greg Wallen verifies this:

> I arrived at the facility at 11:20 a.m. For the next several hours I observed workers, under the supervision of the licensee [LaTorres] and the attending vet [Dr. Dinnes], attempt to return the animal to a supported upright position within its enclosure. At 3:25 p.m. the animal died while workers were still attempting to move him.

Another eyewitness account offers more details. Faso met with the crane operators who were there when he died who later removed Stoney's body. They met on October 4, 1995, at the Instant Replay bar in Las Vegas. During their conversation, as recorded with permission by Faso, one of the crane operators who removed Stoney's body spoke about the very moment of his death. She reports that he said:

> The elephant was lying on the ground sort of groaning in pain. Then the trainer walked through the door and that elephant started chirping and calling to him; then he reached out his trunk to the guy like he wanted to touch him. The guy said, "Cut it out, Stoney," and sort of pushed the trunk away. Then the elephant kind of sighed and then he died.

No more fence building. No more Travis. No more woods walking. After nearly a full year immobile in a windowless shed Stoney had, in the words of Derby who was keenly aware of Stoney's suffering, "died, thank God." No more crush. No more rub sores. No more rotting foot. No more isolation. His life as an individual was invaluable, but his last year appears mostly insufferable, and his death was a release. Great and gentle Stoney was dead and beyond the reach of pain. Without successful physical therapy over his year of isolation, it proved impossible to load him for the planned relocation.

Faso was at Stoney's barn the day he died. Her associates were the ones filming the footage of his barn and his screams on August 28, 1995. She remained on the premises for several hours after the commotion in his barn died down, and the observers outside the shed did not know Stoney had died. Eventually, workers forklifted a dumpster with a bright blue tarp covering it away from the site. The spectators, including Faso, did not know that it was Stoney's carcass inside the container headed immediately to Craig Road Pet Cemetery. Stoney's death was only known to a relatively few individuals, and it was kept under wraps. The next day, when she discovered what had happened, she reacted strongly.

Someone contacted Craig Road Pet Cemetery and gave certain dimensions for a grave of more than fifteen by fifteen feet by twenty feet deep. After it was prepared, he was taken to the pet cemetery and buried. Burial of performing animals is not uncommon. It is the fact that he was so quickly buried without a necropsy that is unfortunate in Stoney's case, according to Derby.

During a necropsy (an autopsy of a non-human body), a vet can learn useful information regarding cause of death and other underlying conditions. Necropsy is a standard, though not required, practice in cases such as Stoney's. The exact cause of Stoney's death is thus unknown because no necropsy was performed. It is likely that given his debilitated and well-known condition that a necropsy wasn't deemed necessary. Perhaps he underwent cardiac arrest from the extreme amounts of stress and pain he was enduring. It could be some other cause.

Derby says he had "had enough and just gave up." Dr. Dinnes made similar comments in the public record. Some posthumous media reports present paraphrased versions of the same sentiment. Derby believes the attempt to move him was an ill-formed plan. She says Stoney would not have died if a crane had not been brought in to attempt to move him. She believes because of this he fell, and the fact that he injured his other leg "was a major contributor to his death." Other parties disagree. The objective truth simply is not available. To my knowledge, no one has suggested that any overt foul play was at hand. When elephants go down, there is always a frantic rush to get them up-righted before their massive weight can damage their lungs and other organs. If they can't rise, they sometimes die from complications caused simply by their massive bulk. Perhaps this is what happened to Stoney.

A cardiac issue may be logical for another reason. One of Stoney's siblings, Tina, ended up at the Tennessee Elephant Sanctuary and also suffered a bad case of foot rot. Upon her death, a necropsy was performed, and Dr. Steven Scott thought she may have had a genetic heart defect that contributed to her death. Having the same parents as Stoney, her genetic cardiac issue could have been shared by her brother. Ultimately, the lack of a necropsy confines us to mere conjecture. Stoney suffers no more, and that must suffice.

Chapter 10

The Advocates

With the 2011 and 2012 events of the Tea Party, Occupy Wall Street, and the Arab Spring heavy on the public consciousness, it may seem that activism is a new thing in America. Of course it is not, and at this point the story focuses on the animal activism surrounding Stoney's death. Animal activism in the West has roots back to Pythagoras, who protested animal sacrifices in religious rites and was apparently a vegetarian. Animal activists are definitely not the new kids on the block in the world of enacting the great human activity of activism.

After Stoney died, Mike immediately buried Stoney privately beyond the reach of the media or advocates in a Las Vegas pet cemetery. The details of any ceremony that took place are unknown, though it must have been either a solitary LaTorres or a small group of friends who mourned and interred Stoney. There was no public service.

Faso was devastated upon Stoney's death and retreated to her home in Las Vegas. As a reminder, Stoney is by no means the only hopeless animal case Faso has worked. She has helped hundreds of animals and tried to help scores more. She has helped Ric O'Barry, PAWS, People for the Ethical Treatment of Animals (PETA), and Animal Defenders International, and has worked with dozens of other individuals and animal welfare organizations in attempts to raise public awareness through media and peaceful, non-violence activism. She is accustomed to the harsh fact of the usual outcome of these animal cases. Often, the animals die before they can be helped, the public is overwhelmingly apathetic, those who contributed to their deaths encounter little legal action, and another day dawns. Faso is a very strong and forthright advocate fully versed in the harsh realities of unpleasant death. Stoney's death was the first time in her animal advocacy life, and the last time to date, she shut down.

Once in her home, Faso turned off her phone and entered a two-day period of little outside contact. She describes her condition as "devastated and heartbroken." She, Derby, Hartgrove, and others truly believed they could help Stoney. In the end, Stoney was beyond help. Faso entered a deep state of numbness, shock, and depression. "I couldn't believe it," she says. "It's like Stoney was a broken down machine to them, and he languished and suffered and died and we couldn't help him." For two days she endured in isolation.

Those close to her knew she was one of the key players in the advocacy ring attempting to help Stoney. The papers and television stations were rife with stories about Stoney during the days following his death. Advocates were protesting, Derby and PAWS were already filing a lawsuit against the trainer and the hotel and making media appearances, and Faso, perhaps the most active, was absent. Friends, who were taking advantage of the media buzz surrounding his death to get their various messages heard by the public, began to wonder if she was all right.

Eventually, Derby got through to her via phone and told her that, yes, Stoney was dead, and, yes, they had work to do. Faso states Derby snapped her out of it with some expletive-laced, very tough love. After being told to pull herself together and prepare to go to work, the fog cleared. It puzzles her to this day; she has never been so physically incapacitated by the loss of an animal she has tried to help. She believes it was the unreality and injustice of Stoney's situation and death that proved almost too much for her to bear. She finally decided it was the disturbing energy, something singularly malevolent, just under the surface of Stoney's case that drove her into darkness. During researching this project, I too encountered this malevolence, and was ensnared by it, consumed and controlled by its powerful despair. Derby pulled Faso out of it. My wife was my redeemer.

Advocates held their own public memorial service for Stoney to pay respects and to raise awareness, and this received media coverage. In fact, the media paid much more attention to his death than his final year of isolation. Beginning with the day of Stoney's death, August 28, 1995, local media showed great interest in his story. The advocates involved supplied their side of the story. Las Vegas local Channel 3's Rikki Cheese's report begins with, "Two dozen people attended an unusual funeral this morning. Mourners gathered to remember Stoney the Elephant with flowers, peanuts, and leaves of fresh produce." The footage depicts the service with Derby and Faso dressed in black. A memorial with signs, pictures, and items included a wreath made of fruit, signs reading, "We will never forget," flowers, and even a small black pyramid embossed with the likeness of an elephant. The report shows it was a clear summer day. The voiceover introduces PAWS, and Derby is interviewed. She says "I really tried to help Stoney, and I really thought to the last minute that I would. I really believe in my heart that Stoney will be the last elephant to die like this." On Thursday, April 2, 1998, the *Las Vegas Sun* printed a picture of Stoney's grave in an article about the pet cemetery. Around the simple headstone are flowers surrounded by a stone border. The caption reads "Stoney the Elephant needed a grave more than 15 feet by 15 feet by 20 feet deep." The scene appears peaceful, much like strolling along streams and woods with a dog named Travis must have been, all those years ago.

An attendee provides insight into the service held for Stoney. About two dozen people attended the service held at the gravesite. The weather was clear, warm, and beautiful, though the mood was solemn. Many, if not all, of the attendees agreed with Ed Stewart and were in mourning for his death as well as much of his life in captivity. The group stayed about two and a half hours. Faso says, "No one wanted to leave. It felt like an odd place for him to be buried even though many other animals were there. He should have been by himself at the top of a hill covered with trees and a pond nearby." She and others were saddened they could not do more for him while he was alive. Many of them reflected Faso's sentiment: "If only we could have been allowed to give him some fruit, veggies, and water to quench his thirst when he was languishing on his knees," one attendee remarked. Sentiments ran high. Symbolic of this, visitors to Stoney's grave (and the memorial gravesite in Pahrump, Nevada, maintained by an organization calling itself "Stoney's Voice") sometimes leave fruit around the small flush-set marker.

Nothing out of the ordinary happened that day. Local media were present, and photographs of the crowd gathered around his grave depict a solemn group. The service went as many services do. Stories were told, words were read. Attendees made plans for the future and placed tokens on his grave. The attendees were people filled with compassion and sadness who had desperately wanted to help Stoney As the service and the cloudless day of blue continued, there was not much talking. People stood, cried, remembered, and thought about the other elephants and animals in captivity suffering other fates far from the indigenous landscapes in which their species evolved.

The mementos left on the grave included the miniature pyramid, signs reading, *Stoney, we love you,* and *Never Forget*, and bouquets of flowers. One mourner placed a wreath made of cabbage, carrots, apple slices, grapes, and raisins with the words, "Too little, too late," on his grave.

Carroll Arnow, the seventy-four-year-old woman who took some fruit to Stoney in his last weeks, was not able to attend the funeral. Carroll said she loved Stoney and was very fond of Mike.

She was deeply concerned and considered herself his friend. Mike presented her with a signed 8x10 promotional photo of him and Stoney. She treasured it. While her friend was languishing, she began making a memento for Stoney in the form of a blanket. She was fond of Mike and believed he was truly trying to help Stoney during his final year regardless of what some people said about him. She also thought the hotel did a commendable job trying to provide for the elephant.

Her blanket was not finished before he died, and Carroll could not attend the memorial. A little more than two months after his death, Faso brought Carroll to Stoney's grave on which she placed flowers and the completed blanket she had made, which had the words "Mr. Magnificent" (her nickname for him) unevenly stitched on one side of it and "Stoney" on the other. She left it on his grave for him, a final gift for her friend. She hoped it might keep Stoney warm. Arnow died in 2001 at the age of eighty. Her obituary reads she was born in Terre Haute, Indiana, and lived there for forty years. She left behind a husband, also now deceased, one daughter, two sons, fourteen grandchildren, and ten great-grandchildren. Living in Henderson, Nevada, when she died, she is remembered as a kind-hearted and very nice person and a friend of Stoney's. Friendship was very important to her. In a letter of gratitude she wrote to Faso, she says, "Thank you for taking me to the grave and for being my friend. I value my friendships. They are very special to me." Dear to her, Linda keeps the card to this day.

Faso closes by writing about the service that she and the attendees "stood there as close to Stoney as we had ever been before and hoped his spirit knew we were there because we cared and did all we could to try and help him." Faso expresses her anguish in her response to the Luxor's letter. Dated September 9, 1995, she cites the key USDA inspection violations documented earlier and closes with the following:

Stoney was rotting away in a sling unable to get away from his own feces. I tried to help Stoney, but no one would listen. After all, he was a used up piece of machinery nobody wanted to acknowledge or talk about. Good-bye Stoney, you are gone but not forgotten. Rest in peace; the only peace you've known.

Lacking much control, she operated the best she could and had no qualms expressing her opinions regarding Stoney to CCE, the USDA-APHIS, and local media outlets. In the years since August 28, 1995, the world has mostly forgotten Stoney. Those who knew of him, however, often report they can never forget. Something about his story deeply affects them on an unknown level; it is difficult to quantify. There is something inherently and especially disturbing about what happened to Stoney and Mike. It seems almost everything that could go wrong for both of them did go wrong. Stoney's friends will not forget him. These people's sorrow and heartbreak may be the most fitting memorial he will ever be afforded, this monument in anguish.

On the day of his death, KLAS 8 produced a story discussing the issue. Gary Waddell and Paula Francis reported on his life and isolation: "Months of suffering are over for an elephant that once performed at the Luxor… Stoney died tonight after falling yesterday morning." A reporter interviews Dr. Dinnes, and he speaks of Stoney's severe disuse atrophy and how that in the end he just couldn't recover from his injury. He says often when this happens to elephants in the wild and in other places, they "just give up and die." Dr. Dinnes is visibly upset and pensive when he says of Stoney that "he just had enough." The reporters tell of his injury received in September of the previous year while images of recent protests of the Luxor and the entertainment industry cycle through. Protestors hold signs reading, *Can Stoney the Elephant Walk?*, *Star Yesterday, Crippled Today*, *Stoney the Elephant: One Year in Misery*, *Stoney the Forgotten Elephant*, *The Hidden Secret*, and the like. Francis states the Luxor did not own

Stoney and paid for a barn to be built in an Arkansas sanctuary. She also mentions that officials had planned the move for the very day he died.

The day after his death, the Las Vegas Review Journal printed an obituary for Stoney It reads:

Luxor elephant Stoney dies following leg injury: Stoney, an elephant who performed in a show at the Luxor, died Monday following complications from a leg injury. His death comes two days after animal rights activists protested what they said was the elephant's mistreatment. The 21-year-old male Asian elephant had suffered an injury to his rear left leg while performing in the resort's "Winds of the Gods" extravaganza in September. Since then, the Luxor has fed and housed him in a large maintenance shed behind the hotel. The Strip resort built a sling-type apparatus to support Stoney so his 7,000 pounds didn't strain his other legs. The hotel had planned to ship the elephant to a sanctuary this week, and veterinarians had hoped he would walk again before making his journey. The Luxor spent $30,000 to build a special barn for him in Arkansas. While working with trainers on Sunday, Stoney's leg went out from under him, said Dr. Martin Dinnes, his primary veterinarian. He died midday Monday after being given pain killers and anti-inflammatory drugs."He wanted to get up, but he just gave in," Dinnes said. "Stoney didn't suffer." Dinnes and Luxor officials denied allegations by the Performing Animal Welfare Society that they "incarcerated" and "tortured" the elephant. The group held a news conference at the Luxor on Saturday demanding that he be sent for treatment at the University of California, Davis.

"We're all sad about Stoney's death. But we're equally sad about his life. He was used and abused for sideshow entertainment and then stored for a year in the bowels of a gambling hall in total darkness. That's not what elephants are for," said the group's co-director, Ed Stewart.

Dinnes said the elephant's quarters were lit and air conditioned, *and approved by an U.S. Agriculture Department inspector. He insisted his patient received the best possible care and lauded the Luxor for spending about $100,000 to maintain Stoney, including importing special oat hay for him to eat.*

"We did everything within our power both financially and emotionally to try to see Stoney through this," said Sarah Ralston, a spokeswoman for the Luxor's parent company, Circus Circus Enterprises Inc. "We're terribly sorry that he didn't make it through his journey. But he really didn't belong here. He just gave out on us. He pooped out."

Stoney was born and bred in captivity and started his show career as a baby. His lifelong owner and companion, Mike LaTorres, could not be reached for comment Monday. Stoney was buried a few hours after his death at the Craig Road Pet Cemetery and Funeral Home.

There was no service.

The Craig Road Pet Cemetery is a well-respected family-owned establishment in Las Vegas that has been in operation since 1979. Covering four acres, it is a beautiful and peaceful site. Mostly dogs and cats are buried there, but birds, spider monkeys, tigers, horses, and other animals as well as the remains of ninety-three humans are also buried there as well as Stoney (The cemetery allows the cremated remains of humans to be buried with pets upon request.) LaTorres chose to have Stoney buried in this cemetery. Presently, a simple marker marks Stoney's gravesite with a likeness of an elephant that reads, *In loving memory of Stoney. A Gentle Giant.* According to those who knew him, this is a true statement. The Nevada-based organization "Stoney's Voice" maintains an elephant advocacy Website that displays research into the deaths of performing elephants. While visiting Craig Road Pet Cemetery in September of 2006, the future founder of Stoney's Voice noticed the elephant's grave. Curious, she was unable to uncover much readily available information on the elephant and began researching. After becoming educated on some of the events of Stoney's final year, she offered to pay for a more detailed grave marker, adding his birth and death dates. Cemetery officials said they could not comply because Stoney's owner wanted no changes. An offer to buy surrounding plots was also refused due to the owner's strict instructions. This led to more curiosity and more research.

This eventually led to the creation of Stoney's Voice in 2008 and the group's quest for information regarding performing elephants who have died and been forgotten. They were offered the use of some land on which to create a memorial for Stoney and took this offer, opening his memorial gravesite in Pahrump, Nevada, on the fifteenth anniversary of Stoney's death in 2010.

The advocates trying to help Stoney also did not consider their jobs finished upon Stoney's death. In fact, the letter writing and public engagement increased. An August 29, 1995, an activist press release states, "Stoney the Elephant is Dead: Luxor Hotel's Hidden Elephant Finally Succumbs." Much debate has taken place between the hotel and PAWS. The hotel clearly states the primary responsible party was Mike LaTorres, while PAWS maintains that the hotel had some level of responsibility since Stoney was on its property. Some blame captive breeding programs, some blame the USDA-APHIS, while others are of the opinion that the fault lies in the ethical climate that allows such activities to exist. Derby points out that audiences enable the industry, which she maintains is sometimes abusive. In fact, most circus people and animal advocates likely have quite a bit in common. Derby, who has been so highly critical of animal performance, stated that most of the people she knows who work in circuses are really nice, interesting, and good people. They simply have a difference in opinion regarding animals used in performance. What should not get lost in the flurry of the blame game are the individual animals. Derby blames the exotic animal performance industry more than the individual trainers. She says in the release that "Stoney's neglect is a direct result of a horrible system... If, indeed, these animals are rare and endangered, they are not being treated as such. Note it is rightly the system, not Mike LaTorres, which is blamed. Stoney's death graphically illustrates how they are really being treated." Ed Stewart says, "While we mourn the death of Stoney, we equally mourn his life." It is very possible many performing animals suffer to an extent, but at least in Stoney's case it is known he did have some measure of happiness in his earlier years, as previous chapters relayed.

The hotel and its parent corporation believe that some misrepresented the facts in Stoney's case. A September 17 *Las Vegas Sun* article, "Hotel was not responsible for the tragedy of Stoney," sheds light on this allegation. It was a response to Janie Greenspun Gale's column also printed in the *Las Vegas Sun* that questioned whether elephants can be used humanely as performing animals. In response, CCE's Sarah Ralston writes:

> While it's clear Gale has the best interests of animals at heart, there are several facts about Stoney's existence that bear clarification. As she noted, Stoney's owner, James Mike LaTorres, was solely responsible for the elephant's day-to-day care. In addition, LaTorres was the only person who had control of and the legal right to decide Stoney's future. For better or worse, Circus [CCE] simply had no control over the elephant's destiny. We could not have turned Stoney over to animal rights activists or anyone else for that matter.

Both the industry's and the advocates' frustration is understandable. There are plenty of well-informed animal trainers and performers who follow USDA guidelines and truly do attempt to give their animals the best possible care. It is quite often these individuals who are most confused by some animal advocates who insist that all performing animals must be retired. This is their trade, quite often an inheritance, and it is not logical to paint all animal trainers with a broad brush. Though abuse sometimes happens, this is not a logical foundation for the unreasonable wholesale vilification of animal trainers. Likewise, the animal advocates who do not demand adherence to their beliefs from everyone else and who approach their advocacy with a true attempt at even-handed logic are often frustrated at the unethical animal trainers as well as the inflexible and under informed animal advocates. This issue must be examined and understood through the lens of changing, subjective perspective. Even if the exotic animal performance industry is categorically inhumane as PAWS suggests, any plan to end it must consider the humans involved as well as the animals. Perspective is important, and Ralston's letter provides more of it:

> Our company paid to have Stoney cared for by two of the world's leading elephant veterinarians. The first, Dr. Mike Schmidt, was present at Stoney's birth 20-odd years ago at the Portland Zoo. The second, Dr. Martin Dinnes, is, among many other accomplishments, the veterinarian of record for Siegfried & Roy.

The September 17 letter directly addresses accusations that the hotel was hiding Stoney in an attempt to avoid negative PR and media fallout:

> It's quite ironic that anyone would view keeping Stoney on our property in an attempt to avoid bad publicity. To the contrary, we realize with the benefit of hindsight that, by not requiring Stoney's owner to remove him from our property, we very likely courted such publicity... unfortunately, despite the best available care, Stoney did not recover. His death was the source of great sadness for all of us at Circus Circus Enterprises.

PAWS and Faso vehemently disagreed with the notion that Stoney received the best available care. The activism increased. The advocates, not mollified, continued engaging the media in the hopes of making Stoney's story better known. The media obliged.

Chapter 11

The Media Fallout

In the weeks following Stoney's death, the media featured a number of articles and letters to the editor and showed much interest in the story. Advocates attempted to take full advantage of the situation and raise awareness. The story also prompted longer investigative articles into the USDA and Portland's Elephant Species Survival Program by the *Las Vegas Sun* and KATU Portland. On Tuesday, August 29, the day after Stoney's death, a *Las Vegas Review Journal*'s story, "Luxor elephant Stoney dies following injury," contained more debate between animal advocates and the hotel's public relations staff. In it, Dr. Dinnes reports Stoney went down and "wanted to get up, but he just gave in... Stoney didn't suffer." Sarah Ralston denies allegations they "incarcerated" and "tortured" Stoney, while Ed Stewart says of Stoney that "he was used and abused for sideshow entertainment and then stored for a year in the bowels of a gambling hall in total darkness. That's not what elephants are for." Tension was high.

These allegations confused the hotel management. Dr. Dinnes states, "the elephant's quarters were lit and air-conditioned, and approved by an U.S. Agriculture Department inspector." Ralston reiterates saying, "We're terribly sorry that he didn't make it through his journey. But he really didn't belong here. He just gave out on us." The article also states that "his lifelong owner and companion, Mike LaTorres, could not be reached for comment." As mentioned, Mike never publically commented on the subject.

Other articles appeared, not always accurate. Cathy Scott of the *Las Vegas Sun* wrote a piece, "Luxor show elephant found dead," which has some mistakes. She writes, "Stoney the elephant was just days from being moved from Las Vegas to the only elephant sanctuary in the country." PAWS did exist, at the time. The title is also confusing. Several people, including his trainer, surrounded Stoney when he died; he was not "found dead." Dr. Dinnes is quoted as saying they were about to move him to Arkansas but were "waiting on a break in the weather." This is also a new piece of information. Perhaps less immaterial is the statement, "Because the elephant's owner...did not have the financial means to take care of Stoney when the income generated from the elephant's shows stopped, Luxor officials agreed to take care of him." When performing animals can no longer earn their keep, so to speak, often their care is downgraded due to the harsh realities of simple economics. Most private performing animal owners do not have entities such as the Luxor to help them pay for their animals' needs. Of course, even with this generous assistance from the Luxor, Stoney's life remained suboptimal. The company could only do so much.

The coverage heated up, and the debates grew fiercer. An article written by Janie Greenspun Gale of the *Las Vegas Sun* is more scathing. Her article, "Where was USDA before elephant died?" launches harsh accusations against all elephant trainers, species survival programs, and the USDA. Gale demands the USDA levy penalties to accompany their violations. She expresses concern that Stoney's trainer wasn't penalized for his many USDA inspection violations and goes so far as to write that the USDA "rarely does anything other than paperwork." The article mentions Derby's legal action: "Pat filed suit against USDA, not for money, but to force it to confiscate elephants currently under control of several circuses and J.M. LaTorres." The USDA does have the power to confiscate, though it rarely employs that power. The article ends with Gale encouraging

Circus Circus Enterprises to join the lawsuit with PAWS against the USDA. They chose not to. CCE's PR Director Sarah Ralston explained via letter that the company's attorneys believed they "do not have 'standing' to participate in a public interest lawsuit..." because "it's unlikely the courts will recognize Circus Circus as a legitimate interested party to represent the 'public interest' in the same manner that PAWS could." Gale believes the USDA-APHIS must have teeth in its violations, so to speak, so animal trainers will be better informed and have a greater understanding of the severity of APHIS violations.

Ralston also writes that CCE is "in agreement with PAWS on several issues regarding the creation of a safe haven system for performing animals that are found to be in distress. We have contacted the [USDA] to voice our support for several elements for the animal inspection reforms being proposed by PAWS." Considering this solidarity regarding certain points, overly scathing articles and responses may have been counterproductive. For instance, Mike H. Sloan, Vice President and General Counsel of Circus Circus Enterprises, Inc., wrote in a letter after Stoney's death to an USDA-APHIS administrator that CCE "believe[s] that a number of the recommendations made by PAWS merit serious consideration... it is clear that there is a common interest among all concerned parties to insure that reasonable safeguards are in place for performing animals such as Stoney." It is most likely that cooperation between all parties will yield the greatest benefit for animals used in performance situations, not divisive hatred and accusatory rhetoric. If animal performance is to continue, trainers, circuses, advocates, the USDA, zoos, and exhibitors should work together to find points of intersection leading to better animal welfare in animal performance situations. Zealotry should be avoided.

Derby's question of why LaTorres' permit wasn't suspended or why he wasn't at least fined by the USDA is pertinent. I attempted to contact the USDA-APHIS. They were uninterested in officially commenting for this book. Dr. Koch was very willing to contribute to this book, but her superiors would not allow her to answer any questions regarding Stoney or his case. This is their right, perhaps, but their silencing Dr. Koch is disappointing considering the White House's transparency promise regarding governmental agencies.

Faso wrote to the USDA requesting commentary regarding Stoney. In the December 15, 1995 letter, Deputy Administrator of Regulatory Enforcement and Animal Care Dale F. Schwindaman writes in response that "in July of 1995, we were satisfied that Stoney was receiving appropriate veterinary care...we were also aware of plans to move Stoney to a facility in Arkansas, where the animal would have been retired from performing." Schwindaman expresses regrets that Stoney injured his other leg and died before this could happen. He says, "A full investigation of the events leading up to this incident is currently being carried on. If violations of the Animal Welfare Act contributed to the death of this elephant, appropriate enforcement action will be taken." Investigators did indeed discover violations of the AWA, and the USDA sued LaTorres in 1997.

Much closer to Stoney's death, more stories circulated. Notably, the media attention culminated in KATU running a two-part story, written and delivered by Sheila Hamilton, in early October of 1996 that ruffled executive feathers at the Portland Zoo. "Beasts of Burden" features Stoney's story and specifically questions the elephant species survival program of Portland's Metro Washington Park Zoo, Stoney's birthplace. Zoo officials took great umbrage at the report. They claimed sensationalized misinformation. The first part of the report focuses on Stoney, while the second part, aired during the 5pm news, features Hamilton pointing out that half of the elephants born at the zoo have since died, while efforts continue to improve the zoo's tracking of elephants that have left Portland. This led Julie Emry, the anchor, to remark, "Let's hope something is done after this," while her co-anchor Jeff Gianola said the report "makes you so damn mad." Viewers were influenced. Zoo personnel were soon taking many phone calls and answering letters from angry viewers who believed the zoo was somehow negligent in Stoney's death. This prompted a response from the zoo because much of the information she reported, it claimed, was out of date and inaccurate.

In a response article, "KATU's Elephant story rattles cages at Washington Park Zoo," published in *The Oregonian* on November 21, 1996, writer Pete Schulberg presents Portland's rebuttal. Schulberg writes, "Born at the zoo, Stoney eventually ended up in the grubby hands of a Las Vegas showman." All freedom of expression aside, this is not a fair assessment of LaTorres.[1] The focus of the article is the anger inspired in zoo officials regarding Sheila Hamilton's two-part report and the response to the claims made within. Zoo spokesperson Steve Cohen said, "It's unfortunate that the priority of tabloid like television sweeps takes precedence over the important conservation work of dedicated zoo professionals."[2]

Schulberg outlines several issues with Hamilton's report regarding Portland's species survival program (SSP) in the article. He writes, "Hamilton never told viewers that Stoney left the Washington Park Zoo 22 years ago, well before the zoo's elephant conservation and protection measures were formulated." Cohen states, "In that era, you didn't have the conservation mindset that you have now." Some people's issues with the zoo stem from charges that the zoo doesn't keep track of elephants after their initial transfer. The current standard practices are much higher than those in the seventies, and the charge that programs like Portland's creating "surplus animals" that end up in ill-equipped trainers' possession, circuses, and other less-than-ideal environments may not be as clear-cut as some maintain. At the very least, more research is needed on the subject of so-called surplus animals, and all facilities should be judged on their current policies and procedures.

Schulberg also writes that "under the current guidelines, zoo elephants can only go to accredited institutions, and the animals must be placed 'on loan' to enable the zoo to recover the animals should events warrant." In fact, the American Association of Zoological Parks & Aquariums introduced the Species Survival Program in 1981, eight years after Stoney was born. The zoo has a strong argument. For instance, when Stoney was born, the Endangered Species Act was only five months old, having been just recently signed into law by President Nixon on December 28, 1973.

Regarding LaTorres' eventual ownership of Stoney, the zoo thought Hamilton led viewers to believe Portland Zoo sold Stoney to the trainer. In fact, Cohen clarifies, he was "sold to a children's zoo in Montreal and then sold again." Cohen says, "Such dealings could not occur under the present rules." In fact, it wasn't until well after they bought him that Sally and Mike discovered he was born at the zoo. Sally says the Hunt brothers told them he was at a children's petting zoo in Canada and had gotten too big for the area. Years later they found out he was born at the zoo. The piece voices other concerns, including the fact that Hamilton reported "the zoo was trying to formulate stricter sales and trade agreements." Cohen says that "strategy, in the form of species survival plans, has been in place since 1986." Also, one of the most quoted portions of the original report is the fact that, since the SSP began, over half of the elephants have died. Cohen rebuts, "the great majority of the deaths of the elephants born at the zoo happened in the 1960s and '70s (well before the conservation measures), which Hamilton did not mention." Of the sixteen elephants sired by Stoney's mother and father, all but three of them died in the '60s, '70s, and the very early '80s. Cohen also takes issue with the fact that Hamilton misquoted Michael Keele, and that she didn't mention that the elephant Chang Dee was traded to Ringling Brothers well before the measures put in place in 1989 that no longer permit such trades.[3]

The reality is that elephant captivity and performing elephants are complex issues not lending themselves well to binary interpretation. Truthfully, the present situation is a gray area with valid problems and strengths along the continuum. Of course, it is most compassionate to err on the side of kindness to people and animals, but even this can lead to unreasonable approaches. For example, some very vocal advocates often demand all zoos and circuses immediately free their elephants. This is not only illogical; it is not the wisest choice. In addition, it is probably not even possible. PAWS, the Tennessee Elephant Sanctuary, and the other American animal sanctuaries and facilities with elephants could not currently support the six hundred or so elephants in the country; though it is certain they would eagerly die trying.

To digress briefly, India has recently released all captive elephants from its zoos and circuses. In 2009, the Central Zoo Authority (CZA) of India issued a statement that the 140 elephants in Indian zoos would immediately be retired to national parks, sanctuaries, and tiger reserves. So perhaps it would be possible to release all captive elephants in the United States in time; however, it is currently an improbable suggestion at best.

Ed Stewart believes PAWS' elephant sanctuary is better than zoo confinement, but even it and its many acres are insufficient. Stewart maintains advocacy should focus on indigenous ranges in Africa and Asia where human-elephant conflicts are decimating elephant herds. PAWS maintains that zoos, with proper space allotments and other considerations, can serve as elephant sanctuaries if they work to provide for the animals properly. PAWS is not anti-zoo, even though many believe it to be. It is possible for some elephants to thrive in some zoos, and the details of this must be left to the experts. Though many advocate that elephants should not be kept in circuses or traveling shows for any reason; zoos, sanctuaries, trainers, and advocates must work together to realize elephants are in captivity and will likely remain so in the near future. The question is what can be better done to meet their needs? And, how can various captive environments serve as acceptable sanctuaries? In a show of growing solidarity between sanctuaries and zoos, the Oakland Zoo hosted PAWS' advocacy event the "Summit for the Elephants" in 2012. Hopefully, this will help usher in this new age of sanctuary, advocate, zoo, and conservationist unity.

On the other hand, some animal professionals dismiss all advocates as uneducated and overly passionate meddlers. This is as unwise as advocates dismissing the knowledge and skills of all animal professionals. Many of the strongest animal advocates were once animal professionals themselves and trained many different species of animal. In addition to Derby's Hollywood experience, the great elephant advocate Carol Buckley trained elephants for performance, and Ric O'Barry (star of the Oscar-winning film *The Cove*) was the trainer of the dolphins used in the '60s television series *Flipper*. Mike and Sally trained Stoney according to the standards of his era. Trainers were taught to chain their elephants for long periods and to use dominance techniques to control them, including the occasional use of the bull-hook that the LaTorreses employed on Stoney. Buckley even utilized these domination techniques before she changed her philosophy regarding elephant handling. Sally Joseph (once LaTorres) states that she and Mike would not have ignored the present information regarding captive elephant well-being if it had been available to them. Even though people interested in the issue of captive animals have strong leanings one way or another, polarizing the issue and getting blindly devoted to one side does little to help humans understand how to care best for elephants. Even more importantly, it does nothing to help elephants.

As for Sheila Hamilton's bold television report on the

situation, reactions are likewise polarized. Some, such as Washington Park Zoo's spokesperson Cohen, believe it was sensationalized and presented out-of-date information with a clear and unfair bias. Others such as Faso believe she is heroic for writing such a prominently featured report and unflinchingly rocking the boat.

After Stoney's death, newspaper articles, letters to the editor, activist newsletters, television reports, television features, and other discussion continued for several months with some remnants resurfacing here and there a few years after his death. Eventually, as always, the media's short attention span was refocused. Other animal suffering issues demanded the attention of animal advocates. Time passed, and the story of Stoney's life lost its edge and began graying toward obscurity. August 2012 marked the seventeenth anniversary of his death. His grave still has the simple marker at the same place in the Craig Road Pet Cemetery, though it is rarely adorned with produce, trinkets, or messages of love and remembrance anymore except by Faso. It still reads, *In Loving Memory of Stoney, A Gentle Giant*. All who learn of him can join in that loving memory, preventing its fading from the Earth. Faso wrote a letter to the editor every year for ten years on the anniversary of Stoney's death remembering him and urging the public not to patronize animal acts. The paper only saw fit to publish the one dated September 1, 1996. In the letter, Faso addresses Stoney directly and tells him that we "didn't deserve your loyalty, your magnificent serenity, or your trust." Stoney's story tells of just one animal that has suffered and died. Stories only survive with active participation of those who listen, understand, and pass them along. And of his story, more pieces remain.

Chapter 12

USDA-APHIS

Recall that the USDA's Mr. Schwindaman wrote in response to Faso's inquiry that "a full investigation of the events leading up to this incident is currently being carried on. If violations of the Animal Welfare Act contributed to the death of this elephant, appropriate enforcement action will be taken." The agency discovered that LaTorres violated the AWA, suing him in 1997.

The charges stated that while LaTorres was licensed and operating as an exhibitor who was fully aware of the regulations and standards, he willfully violated them. The decision and order were filed on July 28, 1997, by Judge Edwin S. Bernstein and is listed as AWA docket number 97-0012. For the two years since Stoney's death, LaTorres had been absent.

Like his divorce proceedings, LaTorres failed to appear at the hearing and was found guilty on all charges. His failure to appear constituted his admission of the allegations regarding the violations of the Animal Welfare Act. The court found LaTorres guilty of failing to provide the following to Stoney: a structurally sound transport enclosure; an adequate shelter from inclement weather; adequate food storage; adequate food; adequate cleanliness of Stoney's primary enclosure; cleanliness of the premises; an adequate written program of veterinary care; adequate removal of animal wastes; adequate ventilation, and an adequate pest control program. The penalty assessed was a fine of $5,000 and disqualification from obtaining a USDA license for five years.

All parties involved seem to agree that what happened to

Stoney was unfortunate and unacceptable. Some parties want to place the blame squarely on LaTorres. Besides him, it seems the most questioned entity in the Stoney affair is the USDA-APHIS. Faso never received an answer regarding her seemingly fair inquiry questioning why LaTorres' numerous violations were never met with penalties or license revocation; neither did Derby. Early action on the agency's part may have prevented Stoney and Mike's ultimate situation, the theory goes. However, it was USDA-APHIS who filed the legal proceedings and at least this provides an official response to Stoney's fate. Again, could it have been possible that Mike LaTorres was massively depressed, lacking support, and overwhelmed? It remains unknown.

One of the positive things to result from Stoney's crippling and death is a movement to ban hind-leg stands and walks in elephant performances. Supporters are attempting to convince the USDA-APHIS to adopt and enforce this suggested ban. Elephants are often injured from performing the very trick that eventually led to Stoney's death. Elephants carry most of their weight on their front legs and only support around forty percent of their total weight on their hind ones. Faso asks in an interview, "when is the public going to realize that elephants aren't built to do hind leg and front leg stands?"

Banning hind-leg stands and walks is logical. The article, "An overview of foot conditions in Asian and African elephants," by Csuti, Sargent, and Bechert discusses details on weight distribution of elephant legs. For example, a large African male elephant weighing 13,200 pounds would have the following weight distributions. When standing, each foot supports 3,300 pounds. During walking, with one foot swinging, each foot supports 4,400 pounds. With only two feet supporting the entire bulk, the two feet would "bear 6,600 pounds, for a pressure of 25.98" pounds per square inch.[1]

A weight study conducted on an African elephant named Angus under the care of Michael Hackenberger at the

Bowmanville Zoo near Toronto is helpful in discussing the problematic nature of the hind-leg stand. The study found the 12,800-pound elephant normally carried up to 60 percent of his weight on his forelegs. Angus was wild, caught in 1979, and died in 2006. At the time of the study, he was the largest African elephant in captivity. A semi-truck weigh station revealed Angus carried about 7,600 pounds on his forefeet. To perform a hind-leg stand, the center mass of the elephant must be reared up and over the hind legs. Only designed to support less than half of the animal's weight, the bones are slightly thinner in the hind legs and they are often visibly more spindly than the front. Free-ranging elephants do sometimes rise on their hind legs to get food from trees, but this is not a heavily repeated behavior over extended periods. During the trick, suddenly one hundred percent of the elephant's weight is on the hind legs, exerting tremendous pressure. Often, the hind legs suffer injuries when this occurs, as was the case with Stoney. Ultimately, it can be argued, the hind-leg balance trick led to his year of isolation and eventual death.

The reader can recall Sally Joseph's arguments with Mike regarding Stoney's performing the hind-leg walk and stand while they were married. She never felt comfortable when Stoney was performing that particular trick, and she was furious when she found out it was this very trick that injured Stoney. The true numbers are impossible to come by, but Derby insists the hind-leg stand and walk injure many elephants each year.

As mentioned, PAWS and other members of the animal advocacy community plan to introduce legislation that would ban hind-leg stands and walks as well as heavily curtail some of the more violent methods of training baby elephants. In the past, Derby and Stewart got as far as a congressional hearing regarding chaining of performance elephants, so perhaps their influence will help spread awareness regarding this particular issue.

Since it appears animals will remain in performance situations into the foreseeable future, PAWS argues it is logical to take steps to reform the regulations regarding their care. Until elephants are no longer used in performance, their care and wellbeing must be paramount, and facilities, governmental monitoring bodies, and individual trainers must be more effectively educated and monitored. This is where the services of the USDA-APHIS are paramount. Exhibitors need close oversight and guidance. The issue lies with the ones who do not have their animals' best interest at heart, and this reason is serious enough to warrant massive reform in the exotic animal performance world. Stoney is among the best and most relevant examples of what can happen in the worst of situations. The outcome of the trial seems to have been a small penalty in regards to what was taken from Stoney. LaTorres let his license expire before the trial and never reapplied. He effectively disappears from record after Stoney died, forever enigmatic. Though the trial may be considered a small victory for Stoney's memory by some, it at least sheds some light on the plight of injured and soon-to-be-forgotten animals used in performance.

As of September 1, 2010, USDA-APHIS has created a team specifically charged with inspecting traveling elephant exhibitors. It is likely Stoney's story has at least partially informed the creation of this special task force. Dr. Chester Gipson, Deputy Administrator of Animal Care with Aphis, writes in a letter to the well-known animal advocate Don McElroy:

> APHIS' Animal Care program has formed a team of veterinary medical officers that will inspect USDA-licensed, traveling elephant exhibitors across the country. The members of this special unit have the necessary experience and skills to fully monitor the exhibitors' compliance with all pertinent Animal Welfare Act regulations. Team members will conduct their inspections at consistent and appropriate intervals to ensure

that the elephants are being properly cared for and handled according to federal standards.

The USDA-APHIS sometimes receives criticism from members of the animal advocacy world. Perhaps the creation of this team was in response to increasing pressure from advocacy groups and increased public awareness and concern. Gibson continues in his letter:

> Creating this team enhances our efforts to regulate this particular group of licensed animal exhibitors. We see several benefits from this enhancement: 1) the team will conduct timely inspections; 2) the Animal Care program will be able to identify problems earlier than in the past; and 3) Animal Care will be able to respond more quickly to complaints.

Each of these three benefits could have lessened Stoney's suffering and prevented his premature death. He also writes that the "work of this team will continue to bolster our efforts to be more consistent across the board with all our inspections, and we will be in a position to better monitor the accountability of these USDA licensees." Again, this seems to speak directly to Stoney's situation. In an affidavit for the trial against Stoney's trainer, Greg Wallen repeats what vets have said as well as elephant care professionals: "[Stoney's trainer] had failed to follow exercise, therapy and medication programs for this animal prescribed by the attending veterinarian." If this unit existed in the mid-nineties, it is very likely that LaTorres would have gotten the guidance he needed and that Stoney could still be alive today. At the time of publication, Stoney would have been around forty years old with, most likely, two decades of life ahead of him. Hopefully, other elephants and trainers will benefit from reform movements such as these within the government. In fact, it is hard not to see the details of Stoney's story as an embedded impetus behind the three benefits stated by Gibson, and perhaps this team will have the support it needs to make a difference.

Chapter 13

Application

When faced with Stoney's story, many people immediately want to assign blame, and blame should not be tossed about lightly. This book is not about that, and I would like to be clear regarding my informed opinion of Mike LaTorres.[1] What happened to Stoney is clearly not his fault alone; he is not a villain. It is also not any fault of the hotel or the parent corporation that employed the pair. I have mentioned several times that perhaps if Mike had more support things would have been different. Clearly, the hotel and its parent corporation offered much assistance to the trainer, so that statement is not critical of them. Any of the attending vets or officials involved in the case is likewise free of blame, as is the regulation-following circus world. It is likely that LaTorres, all the attending vets, the Luxor, CCE, and all other involved parties did the best they could and Mike and Stoney still encountered vast misfortune. The system of overseeing elephant performance has cracks in it that sometimes allow animals like Stoney to fall through. It is not necessarily anyone's fault.

Admittedly, some individuals involved in the caregiving and oversight of Stoney may have made mistakes. However, this book should not be seen as an indictment of them. Ultimately, Pat Derby has suggested that the blame does not fall solely on the individuals and entities discussed in this book; it falls more logically on the shoulders of the patrons who continue to purchase tickets with no inquisitiveness as to the welfare of the elephants in the shows. As a past animal trainer herself, she says that without the audiences there could be no elephant performances. She believes elephants should never be used in any performance situations, but that is often contested. Many humans depend on elephant performance situations, and it is important to remember that their needs must be considered as well. Carol Buckley's statement seems very fair to all parties involved when she writes "ultimately, I would like to see all commercial use of elephants held to a higher standard. I think it's unethical to take endangered species from town to town. It's unethical to put them in the environment that does not meet their needs biologically and physically." As long as they are legally taken from town to town, it is up to the USDA-APHIS to monitor the exhibitors and be certain they are following the rules. A USDA-APHIS spokesperson Jim Rogers (also quoted in the Honolulu Star Bulletin as was Buckley's previous statement) wrote of his agency that "we are watching, and we care how [animal exhibitors] are treating animals and how they are supposed to be treated." Many people believe animals' plights are not priorities. Stoney's story is a jarring reminder that there are often issues with elephants used in performance, and that in spite of governmental regulation and nice trainers with good intentions, much can go wrong.

Some have the following question: "How does animal advocacy affect me in my everyday life?" Faso offers an answer. All people should be devoted animal advocates to a degree with which they are comfortable because if someone learns to have compassion for animals, for species other than their own, it is possible that their compassion for humans will increase. If one truly cares about the wellbeing of an elephant one has never met, one might care much more for the suffering person in the street or in their family. This is not always the case, of course, but it appears a distinct possibility.

A highly endangered elephant dying in his early twenties from unnatural causes is bound to raise other questions. Does captivity actually increase the total number of elephants experiencing a high quality of life? How does captive elephant breeding improve situations in indigenous ranges? Could elephants actually go extinct? And how would it affect us if they did? What exactly would happen? Ecologically, in indigenous ranges, elephant extinction would have drastic results. One of the foremost elephant experts in the world, recognized as the leading global authority on the African elephant, Dr. Cynthia Moss says:

> The ramifications [of elephant extinction] in terms of habitats would be huge. Elephants are the architects of the savannahs. Without them the semi-open areas would be replaced with bush and as such would be inhospitable to many species. In the forests, elephants are solely responsible for the replacement of dozens of tree species. The process of eating the seeds and distributing them are crucial.[2]

Elephants are important symbionts to their natural surroundings. Some trees' seeds cannot germinate until they pass through the gut of an elephant. Debbie Leahy, PETA's Director of Captive Animal Rescue and Enforcement, echoes Moss's sentiments:

> The loss of these species would have a severe impact on their ecosystems and other wildlife that depend on them. Elephants modify their habitat by converting savannah and woodlands to grasslands, keeping these areas open so other species that depend on such ecosystems can use them. Without elephants many other species will be in jeopardy as well.[3]

The complete spectrum of ways in which the elephant extinction would affect other species, the world, and humanity is simply unknown. Humans should study and help elephants. Undoubtedly, a great balance in indigenous ranges would be lost if the elephant were driven to extinction. This says nothing of the much less important fact that the elephant that has delighted and fascinated humanity for thousands of years would be gone. A world in which elephants only exist in museums and fading memories—or only in captive environments—would be one with less wonder. Eventually, all memories of them would fade and they would exist only as a footnote, entries in natural history books not unlike the animated illustrations of wooly mammoths seen in textbooks. As to their conservation, biological needs, and moral consideration, at the very least Faso's opinion that animal circuses and other elephant performance acts in their present state appear to be ill-equipped to provide for them properly seems logical enough to warrant individual research.

Animals in America such as Stoney, even though one may not personally know them, are protected by the United States government and are important. There are laws and regulations in place to keep individuals from falling through the cracks as Stoney did. The public—particularly the elephant performance attending public—could urge the government to enforce these regulations more strongly. Governmental regulations are not a panacea, but they can help. Perhaps they should be stronger and better enforced, but there is a system in place designed to provide care and oversight for animals such as Stoney. It sometimes doesn't work, but it also does not always fail. In 2009, The USDA-APHIS successfully seized Ned the elephant from a less-than-ideal situation and placed him in the Tennessee Elephant Sanctuary where he lived out his final few months with full freedom of movement in a giant natural habitat. If the government hears from the people, it will understand that they are concerned about these issues.

As disturbing as Stoney's story is to many people, some positive things have emerged from it. One measurable effect of his death beyond the lawsuit involves the exotic animal performance aspect of the Vegas strip. As of March 8, 2012, there remains only a single animal act on the strip, a big cat act.[4] Advocates such as Derby and Faso believe the fewer exotic animal performance acts, the better. Beyond possible animal welfare concerns, exotic animal performance often entails some level of risk for the audience and the trainers.

In fact, Stoney is one of three key incidents that have convinced the authorities in Las Vegas that animal acts are not as desirable as they once were. In 1989, the animal advocacy group PETA was involved in a trial involving a Vegas entertainer after he was videotaped slapping and punching his orangutans before going on stage with them. Faso was also involved in this case, and the release of the video surveillance created considerable public outcry. Stoney's death in 1995 was the second key animal incident that escalated public disenchantment with animal acts. Finally, the 2003 incident during the Siegfried and Roy White Tiger show at the Mirage in which Roy Horn was mauled cast further doubt on the feasibility of exotic animal shows. Horn survived the injury, but the Vegas hotels and casinos appear to be much less interested in exotic animal shows. After all, even when managed by competent, caring trainers these shows present a certain element of risk. There is always some degree of inherent danger to humans, be they performers or audience members, in elephant acts. Also, animal advocacy protests ever increase and good business logic often dictates the avoidance of such shows and the managerial headaches they bring.

The reduction of Vegas exotic animal acts can be seen as a positive, as can be the increased focus on performing elephant issues. Thirdly is the increased impetus for eventually introducing legislation that would ban hind-leg stands and walks in elephant performances. Also, one of the key vets in this story provides a fourth element. Dr. Michael Schmidt points out that some positive medical data has been gained. He writes, "On the plus side, a significant amount of information was learned about long-term care of an elephant with severe leg injuries, and this information will benefit other elephants unfortunate enough to sustain similar injury." Regarding Stoney, this is well after the fact, obviously, but perhaps his suffering and lack of recovery can help future elephants suffering from similar situations. Additionally, the innovative crush Dr. Hartgrove designed may be able to help other injured elephants in the future. In fact, a few years after Stoney's death, a group contacted Dr. Hartgrove inquiring if they could buy the plans to his crush. He provided them at no cost, so it is possible his crush design is already helping other animals somewhere in the world.

Stoney also created a greater awareness of performing elephant activism by very clearly demonstrating exactly what can happen if worse comes to worst when a performing elephant is injured. It is currently legal to use animals in entertainment only provided the exhibitors follow strict guidelines. If an entity is using performing animals and is following the guidelines, no one should paint them as villains. It is quite another thing to examine the facets behind the industries one supports and make informed decisions. Advocates can be useful social entities because they call upon citizens to question their role in the captivity of animals. When animals fall though the regulatory cracks, endangered or not, effort should be made to patch these deficiencies in the overseeing system. If one discovers some aspect of an industry that troubles them, one can easily curtail her support after conducting her own research. This book is only one source. Seek out many others before making a decision regarding attending elephant performances and decide for yourself. The United States of America is changing; compassion is becoming more commonplace. Once-accepted bigotries are no longer receiving cultural acceptance. And intolerance is slowly waning. After all, Las Vegas itself has changed for the better. Not only does it have only one remaining exotic animal performance act on the strip at the time of this writing, it is even relatively child-friendly these days.

Who would've guessed?

Part II

The Hanging of Big Mary

"What evil looks had I from old and young.
Instead of the cross, the Albatross
about my neck was hung."
-Samuel T. Coleridge
The Rime of the Ancient Mariner

The Hanging of Big Mary

1916 was a strange time. Big Mary is the only elephant known to have been executed by hanging. Her circus executed Mary in Erwin, Tennessee, in 1916. Her story remains one of the more enigmatic folktales of the southeastern United States. Most accounts seem to focus on the human aspect of the incident.[1] The story frequently resurfaces, having appeared in magazines such as *Popular Mechanics* and *Playboy*, but Charles Edwin Price's brief *The Day They Hung the Elephant* [2] and various other articles are the only published sources of Big Mary's story. Detailed discussions of her life and death are quite few. The spirit of this section is to examine the collected scholarship on Big Mary and present it to the reader alongside Stoney's story.

In 1916, the Sparks World Famous Shows was a small-to medium-sized circus traveling the pre-World War I eastern United States, and on September 12, 1916, it played the booming northeastern Tennessee town of Kingsport. The circus had a herd of five elephants, and Mary was by far the biggest. In those days, a circus was judged by two criteria: the number of rail cars comprising its train and the number of elephants it owned. By either standard, Charlie Sparks' circus was found wanting. Other shows had more elephants and more rolling stock. His show was comprised of a mere ten rail cars (some sources say fifteen) and five elephants, as compared to the eighty-four cars of Barnum & Bailey, which dominated the circus circuit in those days. However, there was another count on which Spark's circus excelled.[3] In those days, the bigger the star elephant attraction, the more successful the circus. Big Mary, it is told, was huge. The circus handbill stated Mary was three inches taller than the world-famous Barnum & Bailey elephant Jumbo and weighed over five tons. She is also thought to have been thirty years old and was valued between $8,000 and $20,000 in 1916.[4]

Circuses were often fraught with over-the-top exaggerations, and on the handbill a drawn version of Mary was pictured next to a human. If the pictures were drawn to scale, Mary would have been over thirty feet tall. She was most likely not bigger than, or even as big as, Jumbo. Circuses in the early twentieth century simply could not be believed as they were masters of manipulation committed to garnering as much profit as possible. Elsewhere, Paul Chambers, the author of *Jumbo: This Being the Story of the Greatest Elephant on Earth*, writes that it is difficult to accept anything P.T. Barnum said due to his infamous showmanship and exaggerations. The leaders of early circuses were concerned with outdoing each other and garnering the most profits possible. Hyperbole was standard practice.

The circus hired a drifter named Walter "Red" Eldridge on September 11, 1916, in St. Paul, Virginia, to work with the circus's elephants as an animal trainer. He had never worked with elephants and was completely ignorant of handling and care specifics. This appears to have been the norm. It was reported he had an immediate affinity for most of the Sparks elephants, though Big Mary worried him. Price writes that Eldridge "had grown fond of little Mabel (the smallest elephant), she was his favorite... Mary was another matter... Eldridge feared her... There was something about her that Eldridge didn't trust— something about her (maybe her sheer size and bulk) made him uneasy."[5] Perhaps this unease agitated her. For whatever reason, Big Mary spooked Eldridge.

The next day, Eldridge was riding Mary, bull-hook in hand, and leading a procession of elephants through Kingsport to a water hole where the elephants could drink and romp. Burton writes that a watermelon rind was near the side of the street, and Mary swerved in an attempt to eat it. Elephants love fruit, something to which any elephant professional can easily attest.

Recall the USDA-APHIS' citation regarding Stoney's access to fruit and vegetables as a major problem during his isolation behind the Luxor. It is difficult to overstate elephantine love for, and need of, fruit.

When Mary turned toward the fruit, Eldridge prodded her with the sharp bull-hook to get her to keep walking. Driven by desire for the watermelon, Mary broke formation and walked toward it. In his inexperience and frustration, Eldridge hit her hard in the side of the head. Big Mary wrapped her trunk around Eldridge, plucked him off her back, and slammed him violently into a wooden drink stand. Then she walked slowly to Eldridge's inert body, lifted a foot, and crushed his head, blood and brains spilling onto the street.[6] The town's blacksmith rushed outside and shot Mary five times with a small gun to no effect. Other accounts report that another man shot her with a .45, only knocking little chunks of flesh out of her, not severely harming her. The remaining elephant keepers managed to get Mary and the other highly agitated elephants back to the circus even though proprietor Charlie Sparks himself galloped to the scene of the death on horseback, only remembering at the last moment that elephants are morbidly afraid of horses. However, the elephants were led back to the circus. Already the crowds were chanting, "Let's kill the elephant! Let's kill him!"[7]

Mary performed later that evening, and all went well with the show. Even so, the townspeople, and the surrounding towns slated to host upcoming circus performances made demands ranging from Mary's destruction to disaffiliation with the Sparks Circus. When Johnson City and other scheduled stops said Sparks could only bring his circus to their town if Mary was not with them, the owner of the circus bowed to their wishes for the sake of profits those future shows would provide. Some eyewitnesses thought Mary wasn't killed simply out of justice for killing Eldridge. Some conjecture that Mary had threatened the owner of the circus one too many times. Others believed she was executed because she was mean and increasingly difficult to handle. However, oral histories are notoriously colorful, exaggerated, and often manufactured. Mr. Heron, the press agent for Sparks Show, told the *Johnson City Comet* that he had "been with the shows for three years and have never known the elephant to lose her temper before." *The Nashville Banner* soon after reported that Mary had been performing "for fifteen years, and this is the first time anyone has come to harm."[8] Regardless, the next day in Erwin, Tennessee, Sparks killed the elephant.

Much passionate discussion centered on how best to kill the elephant. It was known the town blacksmith, Hench Cox, had ineffectively emptied several rounds into Mary as soon as she killed Eldridge. Charlie Sparks said there wasn't a gun big enough to kill Mary in the whole state. Price, however, claims the owner knew an elephant could be killed by shooting into the ear canal. It seems Sparks was trying to save Mary. If it were out of compassion for the elephant or concern for his investment, history is unclear. Some people suggested electrocuting Mary. (Topsy the elephant had been famously electrocuted with Thomas Edison's help in 1903, and the video is available for viewing.[9]) Townspeople bent on vengeance were also supposedly bringing a Civil War cannon to shoot Mary to death. Some believed the best way to kill her was to crush her slowly between two opposing steam engines while some even suggested tying her head to one railroad engine and her hind legs to another and having the trains take off in opposite directions to decapitate her. Sparks agreed to the suggestion of hanging from a train derrick in the nearby rail yard since it was the most humane by his approximation.

This seems suspect. If Sparks knew an elephant could be killed by shooting though the ear canal quite easily, why would he not suggest this when the cries of the village mob ensured her death was imminent? One writer argues shooting her would have been too difficult due to the large public interest in the case.

Craig Dominey, one of the few who have written online about Mary, posits, "Shooting her in the four soft spots on her head would be both difficult and dangerous with the large crowds that would certainly gather around to watch."[10] There are also interesting pictures of Mary on this site. Still, if Sparks cared at all for Big Mary (as some writers clearly claim), it seems logical he would simply shoot her beyond the view of any angry mob, arguably providing her a more humane death. Dominey's position seems shaky, for surely the shooting could have easily happened in private. It seems Sparks could have insisted on a more humane death. Instead, Sparks agreed to the gross spectacle of hanging the star of his show. He even publicized it.

Sixteen years earlier on June 7, 1900, an elephant named Sport was hanged from a train derrick in Baltimore, Maryland. Sport was the big elephant with the Bostock Circus and injured his spine in a fall from a moving railcar while he was playing with the circus' other elephant, Jolly. This hanging, however, was euthanasia. As reported in a special edition of the *New York Times* published on June 8, 1900, Sport was given large quantities of ether to drink before he was hoisted up with a chain, dying in nine minutes after trumpeting loudly and frantically. He was put to death this way after a number of conferences were held to determine how best to kill him. Circus officials believed this was the most humane method of putting Sport out of his misery. There exists one grainy photo of Sport hanging from the derrick with a crowd of men surrounding him.[11] It is unknown if Sparks was aware of Sport's hanging a few years earlier.

Mary did not perform in the Erwin show that afternoon, the day after she had killed Red Eldridge in Kingsport, Tennessee. Instead, she was left chained outside the circus tent. Rumors spread. People said Mary was a demon, a terrible bane, a killer elephant. A Chicago newspaper reports Mary killed seven other men. The *Johnson City Comet*, the day after the hanging, reported Mary had killed eighteen men. A *Ripley's Believe it or Not* cartoon claimed she killed three.[12] Countering these likely fabrications, Hilda Padgett of Erwin, Tennessee, writes:

> In some writings about Mary it is speculated that she was a "killer elephant" that had been sold from one circus to another. That is not true. Mary had been with the Spark's circus for twenty years… Charles Sparks and his wife, Addie, were very caring people. They saw that the animals connected with their show were well cared for. The trainers were instructed to use gentling care.[13]

Dominey's research seems to agree with Padgett's version. He says:

> Mary was more than just a performer to Charlie Sparks. His father had purchased Mary in 1898 when she was four years old, and she had been the family pet ever since. After Charlie married Addie Mitchell, the circus's head cook and animal doctor, Mary, in essence, became the child that this childless couple never had. Charlie firmly instructed his employees to be kind, gentle and respectful to all his animals, especially his beloved Mary.

The three sources Dominey lists in his account are closely linked to the town of Erwin. However, rogue elephants of the time were often sold to other circuses under other names. In opposition, in the book *Wild Tigers and Tame Fleas*, Bill Ballantine suggests this was the case with Mary. He writes she was originally called Queen, and after killing her keeper was sold under the name Empress. According to Ballantine, her name was changed to Mary. He goes on to claim she killed a child before being sold to the Sparks Circus. He writes:

> In the old days, circuses simply hushed up a killing by an

elephant (after all, wasn't a roughneck just an expendable nobody?), then changed the murderer's name and palmed the animal off on another show. Thus Queen, who choked her keeper to death with her trunk, a la boa constrictor, became Empress, a change which didn't deter her from killing five more persons on one bloody rampage. Under a third name, "Mary," she trampled a child during a street parade. Mary, to some accounts, was given a particular send-off. She was hanged from a railroad derrick.[14]

This seems unlikely. Other Erwin-based sources agree and claim Mary was a childhood pet of the Sparks family and lived with their family for over twenty years. There is a photograph of John Sparks with an obviously adolescent Mary dated 1898, for one thing. This seems to discredit the notion that Mary was a newly acquired rogue animal. Steve Shelton, who has also researched Mary, believes she was with the circus for a long time. He writes, "With everything I've read about the Sparks circus and how it was operated, I cannot imagine Charles putting up with a rogue animal."[15] Price's account does not include the information Padgett offers, but he also implies Sparks was not acquainted with Mary for decades. In fact, he states of Sparks: "He probably knew that Mary had killed before—or at least had a strong suspicion that she had...Yes, Sparks was certain of it. This had not been the first time Mary had killed someone."[16] This could be one of Price's admitted flights of fancy, but there is no mention at all of Mary's having been the Sparks' family pet and first wild animal of the circus.

Oral historical inaccuracy is infamously frustrating. In that spirit, two approaches can be applied to the controversies regarding Mary's status in the Sparks family. First, since these claims come from residents of Erwin, one could assume that these kinder stories are attempts to ameliorate the situation, to make the circus and Erwin appear kinder. It is well documented that many people in Erwin would like to forget the whole event and rue the fact the legendary story resurfaces now and then. Ruth Piper often appears in Big Mary research. Fellow Big Mary writer Vannorsdall Schroeder remarks that Piper has made it her mission to memorialize Mary to wash the town clean of elephant blood. Piper believes that Erwin has for too long taken the rap for Mary's death. She writes, "Kingsport, the railroad, and Mr. Sparks are to blame for what happened to Mary—not Erwin. People feel so guilty about it—we've got to release it. It is a sad, sad thing that happened, but we have to let it go."[17] Indeed Eldridge was killed in Kingsport. The execution happened in Erwin simply because the CC&O railroad was located there and had volunteered its equipment, according to J. Brumette's 2011 article. It is important to remember what has happened to these animals that have died under forced service to humanity. Piper may be truly advocating forgetting and forgiving (she does seem sincere), or the true work may be simple shifting of blame. On the other hand, one could also assume that these oral histories from the residents of Erwin are the more accurate versions since they originate closer to the historical scene of the incident, closer to the oral source.

On September 13th, 1916, Charlie Sparks invited the public to the execution following the afternoon matinee show, though no admission was charged. No photographs exist of the crowd to document its size, but most accounts say 2,500 people were present, while one puts the crowds at over 5,000.[18] The hanging took place between four and five o'clock in the afternoon, and the day was dark and cloudy.[19] The other elephants escorted an uneasy Mary to the gallows. She was led to the derrick, and her rear leg was chained to the side of the derrick to secure her while the other elephants were led away. Sparks thought it would be fitting to have the other elephants escort Mary to her gallows, and they did not appear to want to leave her. Price maintains they were led away to a water hole before Mary was killed. Mary was tethered alone to the derrick, and a chain was put around her neck. The hanging began. The first time she was hoisted, struggling, into the air, the 7/8 inch chain unsurprisingly broke. Before it did, however, some eyewitnesses reported the roustabouts forgot to unchain her back leg from the side of the derrick and the sounds of her tendons tearing and bones popping in her rear leg were clearly audible. When the chain broke, she fell to the ground with a sickening crunch, as Price describes it, her hip horribly broken. Schroeder writes that eyewitness George Ingram reported, "It made a right smart little racket when the elephant hit the ground." Price reports the sound of her hip breaking sounded like "a rifle crack and ricochet."

One supposed eyewitness reported that when Mary landed she ran about terrorizing people until they secured the second, this time fatal, chain around her neck. This is highly improbable. As Stoney's leg injury and resulting immobility can attest to, with a broken hip, Big Mary was not running anywhere, nor was she a danger. In fact, she probably sat on her great haunches in much pain and suffering. In contrast, another witness says when the chain broke, she sat down like a big rabbit. A railroad employee ran up her back with a larger chain. This larger chain was placed around her neck, her leg was unchained, she was hoisted again, and her life ended after about ten minutes of suspension and suffocation, though accounts regarding how long she hung there lifeless span from five minutes to a few hours.

The remaining four elephants, with some trouble, were led back to the circus train from the water hole. Once source says, "According to historical articles on the Sparks circus, the elephants trumpeted loudly as they were taken away, sensing that Mary was missing. These same articles claim that it took several performances for them to adjust to Mary's sudden absence."[20] After ten minutes of hanging by the neck, Mary died. They left her hanging for a half-hour, witnesses say. Then R.E.

Stack, a local physician, pronounced her dead.[21]

There is no doubt that the elephant was hanged on a rainy September 13, 1916, becoming the first known to be executed by hanging for killing a human. Apparently, some people want to blame the people of Kingsport. Some want to blame the incident on the inexperienced Eldridge. Some writers want to place the blame on Sparks, while some have passionately defended him and his circus. As with Stoney's situation, blame flies with ease.

The famous picture taken on that misty, rainy day is sometimes credited to Eddie LeSeurer, and sometimes to others.[22] The picture has been contested by *Argosy Magazine,* which refused to publish it upon submission, calling it a fake. Price, however, maintained that it was genuine. It is a bit grainy due to the bad weather that terrible day and has been touched up numerous times, but many believe the photo is authentic. Burton devotes two paragraphs to it in his canonical Big Mary article. He maintains the writer Johnny Childress submitted an article, "Vicious elephant hanged for killing man," which was published in the December 1916 issue of *Popular Mechanics*. The editor wanted a photograph, but the picture was too dim for publication. The magazine decided to use a sketch based on the photograph for the piece. However, the drawing does not depict Mary hanging from the derrick. It shows her being escorted to the gallows with other elephants. Burton reports that Childers says the photograph shows "the huge elephant swinging from the derrick." An Erwin resident present at the hanging says a local photographer by the last name of Mitchell snapped the famous picture, but it developed very dim. Burton writes that in the photograph, "Mary, unnaturally hanging from the derrick with trunk extended, is suspiciously sharper than her background. Incidentally, when submitted by Eugene Harris to the editors of *Argosy Magazine,* the photo was rejected as 'phony.'"[23]

Many of the circus employees were visibly upset. Many circus people reported being extremely sad and were seen crying openly. One circus woman who supposedly had ridden Mary in many parades is mentioned in the literature. Burton quotes another article on Mary regarding an eyewitness who reported "this woman...wouldn't come down and see the elephant die. She stayed in a hotel and cried."[24] Also, the chief engineer of the derrick, Jeff Stultz, did not operate the derrick during the hanging. At least two sources report that he refused to hang the elephant in protest of the proceedings.[25]

After being pronounced dead, Mary was buried in a grave approximately 400 feet down the track. Price reports that the Associated Press later asked the Clinchfield Railroad to exhume Mary, re-hang her from the derrick, and allow them to get proper pictures of her. Thankfully, Clinchfield management did not honor the request. To date no one knows exactly where Mary's grave is located, though it is mostly accepted she is buried on railroad property.

The notion of Mary being hanged for murdering a man may bring to mind the hanging of African Americans during this time as well. Hanging was then a frequently used capital punishment. It is fairly standard that animal trainers entertain audiences with tricks that make the animals mimic human behavior. Roller skating and dancing bears, elephants riding tricycles or walking tightropes, and dogs wearing skirts and prancing around on hind legs display there is a fair demand for performing animals to act like humans during performance. Dolphins will "wave" their flippers at the crowd, monkeys are trained to smoke cigarettes, and chimpanzees entertain while dressed as police officers. Apparently, people love to see animals behave like humans.

In Mary's case, it appears there is a brand of anthropomorphism in the way we punish animals as well. The notion of why Mary killed Eldridge seems not to have been considered by the circus or the ones who demanded her death. The only issue was that she had killed him. The long-standing belief was that if a black person killed a white person for any reason in the nineteenth and early twentieth centuries in America, he or she would die usually by the gallows. Never mind that Mary may have been simply reaching out for some fruit and that Eldridge's lack of training with the bull-hook may have been factors, the elephant had killed a man and she had to die for the crime. Similarly, never mind that the black woman may have killed the white man because he was raping her or her children, white society demanded her death. Many black men fought back when faced with the crushing hopeless racist paradigm that they faced, and many of their acts of violence were self-defense or family defense. Regardless, they were convicted swiftly of murder and sent to the public gallows. The same was done with Mary. The photo of dead hanging Mary uneasily brings to mind similar images of African American men and women hanging lifelessly in historical photographs, who at the time were considered by many to be no better than animals.

This anthropomorphic punishment paradigm nicely links with the anthropocentric attitudes observed in Stoney's situation. If Stoney were human, or even a dog for that matter, many people may have been more compassionately concerned regarding his year of isolation. Stoney brought joy and entertainment to patrons. Then he was injured and evidently severely devalued. This anthropocentrism at the end of the twentieth century seems akin to the anthropomorphism present in Mary's specific mode of execution. Another Erwin eyewitness told Burton, "there wasn't much sympathy for old Mary... most people thought that the elephant ought to be hung—at least I did... she paid for her crimes as anyone else would,"[26] as if the elephant were a human. Animals may be anthropomorphized when it is convenient for them to be so (such as during entertainment or when they kill or injure a human). Mary must pay for her crimes as any other person would. Nonetheless, she was not afforded moral consideration, as any other person would have been. When push comes to shove, human concerns take precedence to the majority of people. Our anthropocentric culture may periodically anthropomorphize animals, lending them convenient symbolic humanity, but it will never give them true consideration as individuals, at least not yet. This is the variation of anthropocentrism that so easily becomes speciesism.

Another writer has commented on this link. Joan Vannorsdall Schroeder writes that a further twist to Mary's story exists in another story regarding Erwin. Erwinian Lanny Phillips said, "Not many people know it, but the elephant's two Negro keepers were also hanged with her."[27] Other residents reflect the belief that Mary's body was immolated on railroad crossties. Burton writes, "this belief... may stem from a fusion of the hanging with another incident that occurred in Erwin, the burning on a pile of crossties of a Negro who allegedly abducted a white girl." It seems these two stories have been enmeshed into an odd synthesis as the years have passed. The circus owners who decided to hang Mary were not from Erwin; the town of Erwin has not forgotten the sad incident. Many of them simply want no longer to be blamed for it.

Mary-related local media coverage of the early 1900s is sparse. Leaving much to be desired, the newspapers of the time report the four less-accepted versions of the incident.[28] First, there is a lengthy eye witness report by William H. Coleman, nineteen at the time of witnessing Mary's death. He describes the incident:

> There was a big ditch at that time, run up through Center Street... and they'd sent these boys to ride the elephants... There was, oh, I don't know now, seven or eight elephants...and they went down to water them and on the way back each boy had a little stick-like, that was a spear or a hook in the end of it... And this big old elephant reach over to get her a watermelon rind, about half a watermelon

somebody eat and just laid it down there; 'n he did, the boy give him a jerk. He pulled him away from 'em, and he just blowed real big, and when he did, he took him right around the waist... and throwed him against the side of the drink stand and he just knocked the whole side out of it. I guess it killed him, but when he hit the ground the elephant just walked over and set his foot on his head... and blood and brains and stuff just squirted all over the street.

A second version appears in the September 13, 1916 issue of the *Johnson City Staff*:

[Mary] collided its trunk vice-like about [Eldridge's] body, lifted him 10 feet in the air, then dashed him with fury to the ground... and with the full force of her biestly [sic] fury is said to have sunk her giant tusks entirely through his body. The animal then trampled the dying form of Eldridge as if seeking a murderous triumph, then with a sudden... swing of her massive foot hurled his body into the crowd.

This account is troubling due to its coloration and supposition of Mary's internal feelings of "murderous triumph." Also, no other accounts even suggested Mary gored Eldridge with her "giant tusks" which, in all probability, never existed unless Mary had been a male. This account also removes all consideration from Mary and is among the most speciesist.

Thirdly, one of the *Johnson City Press-Chronicle*'s staff writers suggested in 1936 that Mary may have simply been bored. The writer reports, "The elephant's keeper, while in the act of feeding her, walked unsuspectingly between her and the tent wall. For no reason that could be ascertained, Mary became angry and, with a vicious swish of her trunk, landed a fatal blow on his head." This obviously differs from the other accounts and was not reported in any known eyewitness accounts.

A final fourth version suggests Mary may have been in great pain. Erwin legend tells Mary had two abscessed teeth, discovered only posthumously. Perhaps, this version offers, Mary was in such pain and suffering from her teeth that when Eldridge touched her with the bull-hook she went berserk. Again, this fourth report is unsubstantiated and impossible to verify. Four versions. No conclusive proof.

In the first quarter of the twentieth century, elephant handlers had little to no knowledge of elephant biology, physiology, psychology, or familial bonds. Major long-term research of elephant families and individuals did not begin until the last third of the twentieth century, and previous elephant lore was primarily ignorant, fanciful stories of magic and Far East mystic hyperbole. Elephant abuse was rampant, and the misconceptions and misunderstandings about the great animals were numerous.

Topsy, the elephant who was electrocuted on January 4, 1903, by Thomas Edison at Coney Island's Luna Park, suffered great abuse. She was executed by electrocution because she had killed three people, including a trainer who had fed her a lit cigarette. Interestingly, hanging was considered as an execution method for Topsy, but after the intervention of the American Society for the Prevention of Cruelty to Animals (founded in 1866), hanging was deemed inhumane. One can only assume the ASPCA was unaware of the situation in the small town of Erwin in 1916.

Researchers such as Iain Douglas-Hamilton, Anthony Martin-Hall, and others have posited that elephants may indeed have an awareness of death. Joyce Poole has written about emotion witnessed with elephants at play. Gay Bradshaw and others have recently argued elephants' famous and long memories and complex psyches may play a role in their developing post-traumatic stress disorder. [29] Many behaviors have been associated with grief, non-maternal mothering, mimicry, art, a sense of humor, altruism, self-awareness, vast memory, and possibly even language. Also, Poole has illustrated the complexities of elephant communication. These now-acknowledged elephantine complexities point to the fact that elephants are far more aware than anyone could have possibly known in 1916. In light of this, it is interesting to note that during the performance the day after Mary's death, the elephants acted strangely indeed.

The elephants performed the same routine they had been performing with Mary for years. The performance went well, but as they were being led away one of the elephants, Shadrack, broke away from the herd. An account appearing two days after Mary's death in the September 14, 1916, version of the *Johnson City Staff* recalls:

> Someone yelled "The elephants are loose," but this was superfluous as the angry snort had already warned the people... women tumbled over, men were knocked down in the wild scramble, hats were smashed... only the hasty capture of the beast by the keeper saved life... many were painfully bruised, but none seriously.

Given the known complexity of the elephant psyche, it could be possible that Mary's unnatural death prompted this outrage.

The facts remain sparse. No one knows from where Eldridge drifted in or if he had family or if anyone missed him after he died. Some believe that he was from St. Paul, Virginia, and was sent there for burial at the expense of Charlie Sparks. There are audio recordings from several eyewitnesses on file at the East Tennessee State University Burton-Manning Folklore Collection, but of the life and times of Walter "Red" Eldridge, no one knows. It is known he drifted into St. Paul, Virginia, one week before he signed up with the circus. In St. Paul he worked at the Riverside Hotel cleaning and doing odd jobs. He then signed up to work with the Sparks Circus elephants, and one day later, he was dead. Everything else regarding him is a mystery.

In the afterword of his book, Price says, "There have not been any large scale works written on the hanging...the few articles written in recent years about the elephant are filled with errors and are clearly influenced by the oral tradition." Price claims the best is the one written by Tom Burton and published in the *Tennessee Folklore Society Bulletin* in March of 1971. However, it is surprising that the article published in the *Staff* the day after Mary's hanging did not mention the spectacle of the murder at all. It was as if nothing had happened, as if Mary never existed. By remembering Big Mary and Stoney as sentient individuals who were forced into an unnatural life and death, one realizes the greater dimensions to life on planet Earth.

Robert A. Nowotny reports, "There is an antique shop in Erwin memorializing... Mary's death. The owners of the Hanging Elephant Antiques Shop sell T-shirts emblazoned with Mary's likeness, which also graces the side of their building." Plenty of people want to retell the story to get the facts straight. Angela K. Brown is one of the few writers to offer anything on the incident. The following is from her article "1916 Elephant Hanging Still Haunts Erwin, TN," which discusses some of the anthropomorphic inconsistencies in the papers of the time:

> Newspaper accounts differed widely and were influenced by emotion and rumors, [Charles Edwin] Price said. In one colorful — but unsubstantiated — story, the sheriff arrested Mary and chained her to the jail in Kingsport before letting her travel with the circus to Erwin. Another account that remains popular but is untrue had the townspeople of Erwin actually putting Mary on trial, convicting her of murder and sentencing her to death.[30]

Though there may have been no actual trial, it is clear that Mary was indeed executed because she killed Eldridge. "When you have an event that happened so long ago, especially something this bizarre, folklore takes over in a lot of ways," writes Price.

Erwin resident Ruth Piper, who has researched the hanging, has tried for years to get approval for a memorial for Mary and to display an exhibit about the hanging. City leaders rejected both ideas. Piper wants an elephant statue and fountain built in town, a movie at the visitor center, and a memorial wreath laid in the railroad yards.[31] "They want to keep it quiet, but it's part of our history," Piper said. "And if it's told correctly, people will understand and won't blame Erwin anymore."[32]

Agreed. The crux of the matter is not about assigning blame for what happened to Mary and Stoney. Tennessee, just as each state of the Union, has plenty of unfortunate stories of bygone eras of which no one is proud. The story should not be told solely in order to reassign blame away from contemporary Erwin. The larger view should focus on Mary, one of the true victims of the incident. That statement also implies no disrespect to the late Walter "Red" Eldridge because he obviously died a difficult death as well. However, if blame must be placed on individual humans, perhaps it should go to Charlie Sparks, who hired inexperienced drifters completely ignorant of animal care to handle ten thousand-pound elephants according to Price. Perhaps not, as this was also, most likely, standard accepted practice and—like Mike and Sally's training received in the seventies—must be socially contextualized. Of course, Eldridge is a victim (as well as any of the people who worked in the circus who liked or loved Mary), but ultimately Eldridge *and* Mary were victims of the ethical climate which accepted, and still does, elephants used in performance.

Scott Plous maintains underlying factors for speciesist behavior, including "power, privilege, dominance, control, entitlement, and the need to reduce cognitive dissonance when committing harmful acts"[33] Big Mary and Stoney can easily inspire one to ponder the captive elephants today that are not yet dead and may be in need of help and compassion. As so often mentioned in this book, all elephant trainers and handlers are not brutal and uncaring people; in fact, many of them truly love their animals and do not physically abuse them. However, some unlucky elephants have been paying the price of their cruel and inconsiderate trainers over the past few centuries in America. Topsy's story is told and Big Mary makes a brief appearance in Eric Scigliano's *Love, War, and Circuses*. In the early twentieth century, James A. Bailey simply eliminated male elephants when they became problematic. The *New York Times* reported in the Barnum & Bailey's 1903 European tour, "five of its elephants were killed for... being 'ugly.'"[34]

Elephants have bent to humanity's will for millennia.

The story since her hanging in 1916 has suffered many embellishments and inaccurate retellings with the main logic of the story often being obscured. As the very few researchers who have spent time chasing down the facts about her death agree, the verifiable facts are always receding further into time. Oral histories are notoriously difficult to verify, and the varying accounts of Big Mary on the Internet and in print are frustratingly fraught with contradictions and varying degrees of coloration. As mentioned, this chapter primarily refers to, and greatly appreciates, Price's work. Price seeks to "replace folklore and myth with logic,"[35] but he readily admits, "that some of the situations in this book have been partially fabricated to fill in voids where facts were lacking."[36] He also admits that during the two years he researched his book he had a difficult time separating fact from fiction. His account is widely accepted as the most canonical one, as speculative as it is. It is also the most considerate of Big Mary as a sentient individual.

Very few of the published versions on the Internet cite sources or attempt to give any ethical theorizing to their claims. In fact, possibly one of the more confusingly crafted accounts implies elephants are vicious beasts and the only reasons one would not want to kill an elephant are sentimental. The 2006 article, after speaking highly of trophy hunters, appears to interpret another

Mary article incorrectly seeming to imply it is unfortunate "that such a homicidal creature [an elephant] would be charitably received at the elephant sanctuary in Tennessee. Where an elephant killed a woman last week." [37] To imply the elephant is homicidal by nature seems unfounded. Of course, circus and zoo history is rife with tales of elephants rampaging and killing humans, and elephants have killed humans in their natural habitats. However, to cite this without giving due examination to the possible confinement, abusive training methods, and damage to their psyche that comprehensively culminated in the rampages—or even worse to dismiss the elephant psyche altogether—is simplistic. It appears some people of Erwin want to blame the people of Kingsport for the hanging of Mary, but that shouldn't be the case. As with Stoney, it is the culture that accepts elephant performance that needs to bear the blame, not the individuals involved. Erwin should not be blamed, or Kingsport, or the circus in which Mary traveled. That point should be emphasized. Mary's hanging has haunted Erwin, Tennessee for almost a century. For once and all, Erwin should be released of the blame they have unfairly shouldered for so long. Charlie Sparks, the circus owner, made the decision to end the elephant's life in the manner of hanging. Erwin is, and should be considered, blameless. Individuals should simply question the industries they support and be reasonably certain that they are compassionate and considerate of all their employees, humans and non.

One unfortunate aspect of the evolving story is the pejoratives Mary has acquired over the years. The original *Sparks World Famous Shows* flier simply bills her as "Mary: The Largest Living Land Animal on Earth" [38] Robert A. Nowotny says it was reported she was talented in many ways. The circus supposedly billed her as being able to play over twenty-five songs on a musical horn and was even the pitcher for the circus baseball team with a batting average of 400. Whatever she actually could or could not do, after she killed her unskilled handler she became known as "Murderous Mary," "Mighty Mary," and "The Killer Elephant," and such. The people in whose care Mary was placed were simply unskilled, uneducated, and ignorant of the vast amount of information now understood regarding elephants and proper elephant care and treatment. Even during Stoney's first thirteen years, the standard practice for elephants in the '70s and '80s accepted almost constant chaining and frequent physical violence. The interesting part of Big Mary's story may not be that she was killed and bestowed with an unearned reputation that has lasted nearly a century, but rather that it appears Big Mary was possibly killed simply because she was hungry and wanted a piece of fruit.

Big Mary and Stoney should be remembered. It is not the spectacle of the hanging that makes Mary's story worth telling. It is also not the year of isolation that makes Stoney's story worthwhile. It is the stories of an abused and misunderstood animal that are important as well as understanding what can go wrong when certain circumstances occur. Stoney had performed the hind-leg stand, most likely, hundreds of times. September 23, 1994, was simply one time too many. Trainers walk elephants through crowds with children easily within trunks' reach today just as Mary was walked through them in 1916. She happened to see a piece of fruit. It could easily happen today.

The Amboseli Elephant Research Project headed by Dr. Cynthia Moss has been studying indigenous elephants in Africa for almost forty years. It is the longest running elephant study to date, and the Amboseli elephants in Kenya are the most celebrated in the world. Dr. Moss is widely considered the leading world expert on the African elephant. The Amboseli Trust for Elephants' statement regarding elephants in circuses is illuminating. ATE's research staff consists of the leading elephant professionals in the world with a nearly combined 300 years of experience working with elephants in the wild and in various captive situations. The group includes Dr. Poole, Dr. Harvey Kroze, and others. If anyone has the proper background to voice opinions regarding elephants, it is these professionals. Consider the elements in the following passage that bring to mind the needs and fates of both Stoney and Big Mary:

> It is our considered opinion that elephants should not be used in circuses. Elephants in the wild roam over large areas and move considerable distances each day. They are intelligent, highly social animals with a complex system of communication. An elephant family is led by the oldest female—the matriarch—and is bonded by kinship, affiliation, experience, great loyalty and affection. No captive situation can provide elephants with the space they need for movement or with the kind of social stimulation and complexity that they would experience in the wild.
>
> Elephants in circuses are bought and sold, separated from companions, confined, chained and forced to stand for hours and frequently moved about in small compartments on trains or trucks. They are required to perform behaviors never seen in nature. In short they are treated as commodities, as objects to provide entertainment for humans. The circus experience has nothing to do with the reality of elephant life and behavior.
>
> In order to keep elephant behavior under tight control in the close proximity, "hands-on" conditions of circuses, it is necessary for a handler to establish and maintain supremacy. Domination of such a large animal must unavoidably involve an element of cruelty, often including the liberal use of an ankus—a bull-hook euphemistically termed "guide" by those in the business, a whip or an electric prod. Elephants have extraordinary memories and it has been demonstrated that they never forget rough treatment by human handlers. Consequently, they can pose an unpredictable and abiding danger to the public, to their handlers, and thus to themselves.
>
> We believe that such intelligent, socially complex and long-lived animals should be treated with respect and empathy. An elephant's

place is in the wild with its relatives and companions. The totally unnatural existence of captive elephants in a circus, which includes significant physical and emotional suffering, is a travesty. To allow this practice to continue is unjustified and unethical.[39]

Others disagree. The sole observation of this book is that it appears unlikely that elephants can be used in performance and have their physical, biological, and social needs completely met. Each captive situation differs, but it seems likely that circuses and single-owner performance situations sometimes have great difficulty providing optimal environments for elephants, no matter how well intentioned they may be. The great responsibility of the consumer is to become educated and make one's own decisions. Also, it never hurts to attempt to decrease suffering, and embrace compassion whenever possible as time marches on, and the beautiful world Stoney and Mary both once walked continues to spin, with myths unfolding.

Epilogue

Further Adventures in Elephant Advocacy

Unlike the people directly involved with Mary's story, some of the players in Stoney's story are still under the giant sky.

Linda Faso remains extremely active in animal advocacy in the Las Vegas area. She is constantly helping other advocates, investigating animals in danger, and helping animals whenever she can. She still focuses on animal circuses, demonstrating against them and animal trainers with histories of abusing their animals. She keeps track of the people on the Vegas strip with animals and people with exotics in her area through USDA-APHIS inspection reports, newspaper articles, and feedback from local activists. She also keeps up with the dolphins "stuck at the Mirage Hotel in their small cement fishbowl with nowhere to go and nothing to do," as she puts it. She tirelessly documents incidents in and around Las Vegas involving animals and provides information to media outlets, most notably after the 2003 Siegfried and Roy mauling. She is still trying to help some animals in a three-acre roadside zoo near Vegas and networks extensively with PAWS, PETA, HSUS, Animal Defenders International, and many others on different animal-related issues. She regularly attempts to get stronger laws for animals passed in Nevada and actively lobbies state legislators, county commissioners, city council people, animal control, and anyone else who may be able to effect change for the animals living around her.

Her energy is seemingly limitless. After all these years of working in this highly politicized and charged arena, she says she is "just getting started." Being quoted at length in the *New York Times* and going viral in October, 2013, she might be right. Though she no longer writes her annual letter on the anniversary of Stoney's death, she says she will remember him forever. Also, she visits his grave annually on the anniversary of his death to remember one of the worst cases she has worked on to date, and to remember the elephant she never met. Now, more than seventeen years later, Faso is as active as ever, attempting to help animals in Las Vegas and elsewhere through her local, national, and international web of legal, legislative, and celebrity animal advocacy contacts. Though emotionally challenged and upset regarding every case she works, to this day nothing has affected her with the bleak hopelessness of Stoney's death and the two days thereafter. On the seventeenth anniversary of Stoney's death, she brought produce to Stoney's grave and spent a few hours in silence as she always does.

No one else was there.

Pat Derby remains the President of the Performing Animal Welfare Society and maintains campaigns, media contacts, and dozens of other global projects while keeping elephants close to her heart. As of publication, she is planning to introduce legislation banning hind-leg stands and walks in elephant performances and reforming baby elephant training methods. PAWS has come to the conclusion that there is no humane way to train and perform animals. They are convinced that the system, based solely on economics, precludes it. They are currently working with Animal Defenders International in forming legislation focusing on traveling animal acts. Derby believes changing public perception is the single most important act an animal advocate can do. Through legislation, PAWS sees opportunities to educate a large swath of people of all walks of life. The ever-growing ARK 2000 sanctuary is in Galt and the Amanda Blake Wildlife Refuge in Herald, California, all three operated by Derby and her partner Ed Stewart. She tirelessly advocates for all animals, but Stoney occupies a singular place in her heart and her mind. She still can't talk about Stoney without emotion. He and his effect on her life persevere.

Derby was heavily affected by Stoney's death. As expressed in local media outlets, Derby truly thought they could help Stoney recover. Upon his death, she responded with her typical furious energy directed into her letter writing to places such as the hotel's administration, the USDA, and local media sources. She was outraged that in spite of various and repeated USDA inspection violations that LaTorres was allowed to keep his exhibitor's license. Another lengthy letter asking why the agency did not respond with penalties or license revocation never received an answer. She cannot speak of Stoney without becoming emotional, her outrage still close to the surface after these long years. Stoney's death has shaped the direction of PAWS' ARK 2000 elephant, tiger, and lion sanctuary in the form of a planned memorial on the premises as well as helped begin the Bucks for Bulls campaign. His death has also lent power to PAWS' more than twenty-five-year commitment to helping bull elephants in peril. Most elephant sanctuaries feature female elephants because bulls have certain needs that can be more difficult to meet due to increased size and periodic musth aggression.

PAWS is also planning to build a conference center with a nature trail around it called "Stoney's Grove." The Website states that "A trail leading from the Conference Center through a boulder strewn oak grove will be named 'Stoney's Grove' and be dedicated to the memory of an Asian bull elephant, Stoney, who suffered and died while performing at a Las Vegas casino. His story will be told along the trail and will illustrate the mistreatment of captive elephants that PAWS is dedicated to ending." Derby, Stewart, and PAWS' efforts continue to escalate and be ever-more influential in the world of animal advocacy. As any outspoken organization will do, Derby and Stewart have attracted some detractors, but with their determination, time, and generous support from Bob Barker, Kim Basinger, and many other donors, they continue to be able to carry out their mission. The memory of Stoney remains clear and forceful in Derby's. She honors him with her life's work.

Ed Stewart remains with Derby, overseeing the daily operation of PAWS. Spending much time caring for their newly acquired pride of lions, retired from Bolivian circuses, it is he who reminds all that while he mourned for Stoney's death, he equally mourned for his life of captivity and limited mobility. PAWS itself remains committed to working with the zoo industry in order to discover the best possible captive environments for elephants and other animals and how to implement those environments. It currently has over fifty thousand members.

Sally (LaTorres) Joseph's reactions to Stoney's death were extreme. As previously mentioned, she was essentially Stoney's mother and guardian until age thirteen. Stoney was twenty-two when he died, their separation lasting almost a decade. She only saw Stoney once after the split in 1988, and having to leave Stoney when she did remains her neck-hung albatross.

When she learned the cause of Stoney's lameness, she was furious. Recall that when she was married to LaTorres, the hind-leg walk was always a point of disagreement between them. She did concede on the point, but was unhappy about it, even when Stoney was a young teenager weighing much less than his adult weight. That particular trick causes many elephants to have rear leg damage according to Pat Derby.

Upon learning of Stoney's injury, Sally reports she was "upset beyond belief." A friend called her with the news of his death, and she immediately felt responsible even though she had had no contact with the elephant for almost a decade. She says, "Stoney had always been a good boy for me and he deserved better." This escalated near the level of self-torture. She says:

I beat myself up on a regular basis that I did not do more for him…if I knew then what I know now, many things would have been different and maybe Stoney would still be with us. I am not naive and know that as an Asian bull elephant, he should have been in a facility that would have let him be in protected contact with some room to roam.

Sally Joseph is now remarried and working as an animal professional in a non-performance capacity. What happened still haunts her. She says with honest candor that overall, Stoney "did not have a good life, and I hate myself for that. I hate that I did not do more for him because, at that time I just did not know what I could do." In reminder, when the divorce occurred, she wanted to take Stoney with her but lacked sufficient resources to do so. It was a dark time, and she could barely take care of herself. She has moved on with her life, but it is clear the memory of Stoney is a dark wound she will carry for a long time, if not forever. After her divorce from Mike, she began working with zoo elephants and has become a dedicated animal advocate and an advocate of protected contact. Sally no longer works with elephants, but in her elephant life after Stoney she became educated and a supporter of non-aggressive protected contact and non-dominance-based training techniques. Stoney's death turned her away from the circuses and into a more nuanced and aware elephant professional, she says. As it stands, she may be the person still living who has been most altered because of their contact with Stoney.

Upon hearing of Stoney's death, she drove to Las Vegas to find LaTorres. Her blind-anger intentions were not good, and it is fortunate she was unsuccessful in her search. Stoney is dead. However, Sally Joseph should not carry the guilt that she does regarding leaving him. She provided, possibly, the best times Stoney ever had back in those easy days of exploring and woods-walking, the very best times of his life.

After her divorce from Mike in 1986, she worked with elephants in several zoos and worked briefly at an elephant compound in Illinois. In 1993, she moved to Tacoma where she began learning the positive potential of protected contact in improving the quality of life of difficult elephants. During this time, she met and married Brian Joseph, a veterinarian. With him, she has two grown stepsons. She left working elephants when the family moved to northern California in 2002. Brian is a consulting zoo vet, specializing in marine mammals, who also serves in the Army Reserve Vet Corps. Sally currently shares her life with four domestic animals: a giant Schnauzer, two Bernese Mountain dogs, and one house kitty. She still loves her boy Stoney, and continues to carry his memory through her days. It is also known what became of Stoney's best friend, **Travis the Border Collie.** Sally reports:

> Travis stayed with me and lived to be fourteen. He was my companion and friend, and I would have been lost without him all those years. He was always happy and ready to go on adventures and always ready to protect me. Though it was his time, his passing was difficult for me. He was peacefully euthanized in my arms as I told him how much I loved him.

James Michael LaTorres is something of a mystery even now. He was the person who was with Stoney the majority of his life, and unbiased sources were all but impossible to come by. Limited details about him have been verified. After Stoney's death, it appears LaTorres apparently lost all interest in the elephant performance business. From the date of Stoney's death, he effectively disappears. His marriage after Sally also ended in divorce, according to Sally Joseph. All that is known of his death is that he died of cardiac arrest sometime in 2002 while he slept.[1] However, information does exist that speaks to what kind of person he was. His good qualities mentioned earlier by people who knew him were reflected by Sally Joseph's final interview for this book. She reported in the interview how she remembered him. She says they had some serious differences in life philosophy and approaches to Stoney. Of Mike, however, she remembers:

[He] had a good sense of humor and was quick to laugh. He was easygoing and non-confrontational, and he was not a hot head. He had many friends, would always be one of the first to help someone, and was ready to lend a hand without question. He was bright and well-read and enjoyed lively conversations. He was open-minded and accepting of all people.

This open-mindedness and his tendency to accept all people are important after reading his and Stoney's story. Mistakes were made, but Stoney's life was not always misery, and LaTorres is no mustache-twirling villain as some animal activists have tried to portray him. His role in this story is complex. Good people often make bad mistakes, and from the input of everyone who was interviewed for this book who actually knew him in any personal capacity at all, it appears this is the case with LaTorres. They remember him as a good person. In the context of the time, Mike LaTorres did a good job taking care of Stoney throughout the many years preceding Las Vegas. Sally reports he did discipline Stoney when needed, but he never overtly beat him or abused him. In the seventies and eighties, there were a plentitude of elephant handlers and trainers who were not as skilled as he was. It's easy to hear some stories and get angry at animal trainers. Unfortunately, I even called him abusive in an article I wrote years ago before I had all the facts, the benefit of years of research. I have since retracted the statement through the publisher and apologized. My current informed opinion is as it appears in this book: it appears LaTorres did the best he could throughout the years and was simply massively overwhelmed during the final year of Stoney's life. The fact that he was a kind person illuminates a point regarding captive elephants in performance that bears repeating. Even the best-intentioned individuals are likely ill equipped to care properly for the staggering needs of an elephant, especially a bull elephant. Moreover, if that elephant becomes injured, the burden is near impossible for one person to carry. Stoney and Mike's stories display, in tragic measure, what can happen when a chain of negative events happen with little support or relief. The debate will continue, but whatever mistakes LaTorres made are long in the past as far as I am concerned. They should be forgiven, studied, and learned from as we go forward into a better world for animals and humans.

The police contacted Sally Joseph after Mike's death. They told her the cause of death and inquired if she knew of any family that might want to claim his remains. She recommended a sibling. The officer left, and nothing else is known. I attempted to contact several of his family members in hopes of providing more perspective and insight into the showman and trainer. As mentioned earlier, I located only one family member, and the interview request was declined. We simply don't know how Mike took the death of Stoney, and it is unfortunate that he could not be better represented in this book. It has been my intention to represent him as fairly and as accurately as possible; this has been done in good faith and to the best of my ability. He is gone, his elephant is gone, and the majority of their stories are lost with them.

Thomas Hartgrove continues with his veterinary practice in Las Vegas and the state of Texas. He remembers Stoney as the case that made him more seriously consider animal welfare. Profoundly affected by Stoney and what happened to him, he did not understand that Stoney would be treated like a "broken-down machine," as Faso puts it. He tried his very best to help Stoney and was shocked that his advice was largely ignored. He will be remembered as one of the people who earnestly attempted to help the suffering elephant the most. Well-respected in his profession, he thinks of Stoney often.

Stoney's Voice continues their campaign to monitor and report on the status of performing elephants in the United States. They remain active in attempting to get the gravestone marker at Craig Road Pet Cemetery updated with more details. Since this has been unsuccessful, they acquired the use of some land in Pahrump, Nevada, to erect a "Memorial Gravesite" for Stoney. They enacted this aforementioned plan on August 28, 2010 (the fifteenth anniversary of his death) and held a memorial service. About a dozen adults and several children attended the memorial, and many people mailed in items from across the country to be displayed at the site. In the three months following the service, more than fifty people traveled to the site to pay respects to Stoney's memory. Most of them leave some sort of trinket behind since his story has affected them so deeply. Everyone who visits and hears his story vocally promises circus nonattendance. Stoney's Voice has also been working with other elephant advocates with their protests of animal circuses in the Las Vegas area, and they continue to educate people regarding the plight of captive elephants.

On Christmas of 2010 and 2011, a small tree decorated with elephant ornaments adorned the site. The memorial is a permanent one, and there are no restrictions as to what can be placed at it. Stoney's Voice plans on maintaining the memorial. They are conducting fundraising in order to purchase more ornamental fencing and an elephant sculpture for the honorary gravesite. They say it is their hope that Stoney's memory will be "kept alive through this memorial."

And Finally

Humanity has many love affairs with mythology: Brave Achilles, Breaker of Armies; Athena and her storm-gray eyes; Circe of tempting danger and mystery; Zeus, who wields lightning. The gods and the heroes only persevere in our memory, the only immortality available to them. And what of our hero? How should Stoney be remembered? An offering to that end:

Torn tendons, the crush, standing in feces, months in darkness, painful lesions, isolation, bull-hook wounds, confusion, lack of physical therapy, falling and the inability to rise ever again, and the like are not the way to remember Stoney. Those are ways to remember the importance of compassion, to remember our humanity, and to ensure Stoney is the last elephant to die in such a difficult and savage manner.

There is a better way to remember Stoney. Recall some of Sally's sylvan memories of Stoney during better times during his younger years. Or recall the memories of those who had contact with him. Las Vegas dancer Ottavio Gesmundo shares these reflections. Of his brief contact with Stoney while working at the Luxor in the *Winds of the Gods* show, he says:

> In between shows we would eat at the employee dining hall, and I would always bring him back fruit, usually an apple. He was very kind, but also had a sense of humor about him, and if I had forgotten to give him fruit he would toss me off his tusks during the scene and the stuntmen would have to lift me up and place me on again to finish the circle around the arena... Once I remember asking Mike if I could bring him a watermelon because I wanted to see how he would react to that. He agreed, and it was wonderful to see. He was

trumpeting with delight when I rolled it over to him. At first he just pushed it around with his trunk until stepping on it and busting it open into several pieces. Then he would scoop them up into his mouth. It was really great. Needless to say he didn't toss me off his tusks that night.

A photograph exists of Ottavio with Mike and Stoney in Las Vegas before the injury. In it, Ottavio and Mike are both smiling huge smiles gathered around Stoney who seems to be peering inquisitively into the camera. It is best to remember Stoney in the joyful parts of his life. His early death was suffering and possibly even preventable, but his life did have happiness at other moments, quite a bit of it. It was not always a caravan of despair. Ottavio's clear position is that animals still have a place in entertainment as long as they are treated fairly and humanely and regulations are followed. He believes that as long as there is no abuse, rewarding relationships built between people and their animals and performances can be educational. Others, such as Faso and Derby, strongly disagree.

Of Stoney's life, maybe we should remember those days that he would possibly choose to remember if he were still alive. Those days in Florida when Sally and Mike would take Stoney on slow walks through the five acres of their property, wind gently blowing over his broad gray back. Or those soft nights when Travis the Border Collie would sleep between his feet with the couple just through the walkthrough, love surrounding him. Or when Sally would sit down and let Stoney graze on tall grass and slowly walk about, his heavy, healthy feet depressing the spongy earth. Or during the off-season on long afternoons when Stoney would help Sally and Mike build fences under limitless skies and play with Travis or chase the unimpressed ponies of those easier years. Maybe we should recall Stoney slowly strolling through the loud summer dusk looking at the fireflies all around him. Or the day at the old Key Biscayne Zoo, Stoney in the bright sun splashing, playing, and proudly holding aloft the priceless tricycle found in the pond.

Intelligence should not be a gauge for valuing non-human animal life, but it remains that many people most value animals (and humans, for that matter) they perceive as intelligent. Elephants are quite popular. Ultimately, if the observable intelligence, psyche, and likeability of the elephant are not enough to convince humans to help it, if that wondrous and venerable creature cannot be saved, the rest of the animals may be beyond all hope.

We can see ourselves in the plight of the elephant who walked the Earth when it was young; we can find common ground. We can care about Stoney and Big Mary and remember them just as we hope we will be remembered and not forgotten. Once we are gone, and our children, grandchildren, and anyone who ever knew us are dead, it will be as if we never existed unless humanity tells our stories. Our names will be among those that are, as Virgil wrote millennia ago, *lost to the dark depths of time*. We should not forget Stoney and Big Mary; they are too big to forget. This book is an insufficient monument to their singular lives.

If only one story of Stoney's myth is to survive the coming ages, maybe the best way to remember him is the day of exploration when Sally, Stoney, and Travis ran together through forests, all three young and alive, down canyon trails and back up again as the hopeful sun rode high in cloudless blue. Think of Stoney: Friend of Travis; Stoney: Builder of Fences, Chaser of Ponies, Eater of Watermelon. Think of Stoney: Canyon Runner. Think of all these things. And remember.

Afterword

By Linda Faso

I first heard of Stoney in mid-April 1995 and was totally unaware of the painful journey I was about to undertake. The caller was vague and not clear on specifics but had heard about the elephant from someone who worked at the Luxor Hotel, here in Las Vegas. Coincidentally, I was working on another crippled elephant named Jenny who was dumped by a circus at a run-down facility outside Las Vegas. To further complicate matters, I was in the process of working with a local investigative reporter on a two-part story about the dangers of elephant rides. I gave the caller information on how to contact USDA and verify if this was true, at the time thinking there is probably a mix up and this is about Jenny. She got back to me a couple of weeks later and said a USDA official reported all was in order and he was being taken care of. I immediately called Pat Derby at PAWS and discussed what we should do first. No one was talking, and it quickly became clear that information was going to be scarce. I contacted and spoke to the inspector handling this case who I had known for years. He was very guarded with any information and mentioned that he had just inspected Stoney and was on top of this. I immediately sent for the report hoping to find out what was happening. I saw signs that he was in trouble and decided to let the hotel and public know about Stoney by doing a protest in front of the hotel and alerting the media. As always, a PR person was assigned to handle the public and the media.

In the next few weeks I tried to meet with executives at the hotel to no avail, so we started a letter writing and telephone campaign to make them aware that the public wanted to know what was going on. I found out which building he was in and monitored it as best I could, asking questions of anyone who seemed to be working close by. I soon learned he wasn't getting the proper medicine, medical care, food, or therapy that he needed. He seemed to be treated as a broken down piece of machinery that had outlived its profitability. In fairness to the hotel, I know they accepted the reports given to them; they believed he was being taken care of. No one would listen to Pat or me regardless of the many phone calls and letters pleading with various officials to sit down and discuss the situation. I was concerned that Stoney was rotting away in the dark. I believe this because when we had the facility under observation, we would daily observe Stoney's trainer go in the door and turn on a light switch. I couldn't stand it that he was in the dark alone for so much of the day. It just wasn't right.

The USDA was well aware from past experience with Pat and me, that we were not going to go away, so they stepped up with more information on their inspection reports. Stoney was standing in feces and urine most of the time, which caused his foot problems. His muscles had atrophied, and he had no access to water unless the trainer went in to let him drink from a hose. I also discovered through investigation that the trainer had taken a job as a security officer further down the strip at a small casino. This meant he was gone for at least ten hours a day leaving Stoney alone in a windowless building with no access to water standing in feces and urine for most of the day. I couldn't accept this. Something had to be done. At some point, the hotel learned about Stoney being alone for so much of the day and put LaTorres on their payroll so he would be able to take better care of Stoney. They must of known at this point things were going horribly wrong with a crippled animal that was injured in their showroom and was now isolated on their property rotting away.

We knew he was slowly dying and the hotel arranged to send him to Arkansas. Pat and I knew even if they somehow got him

Afterword

into his trailer he would never survive the trip. I got word from an insider that they were going to make the move within the week. At that point, I nightly sat in my car until the wee hours of the morning to monitor any movement. I was not going to let them move him without me as a witness, I owed that much to Stoney. I also later learned from a security guard that they were concerned how he would react to sunlight as he had been in solitude in that building for almost a full year.

Next to the building housing him was a trailer park, so my friend and I went and rented a trailer and put it on the lot opposite the building where Stoney was wasting away. Pat sent a couple of people to stay in the trailer and keep a 24-hour watch for a few days. They were the ones who recorded his cries the day before his move was to take place.

When the volunteers had to return to their lives, I volunteered to stay in the trailer around the clock to bear witness. My dear husband understood and knew how important it was for me to see this through. I was ready to move into the trailer and my daughter Angela would bring me food for as long as I needed. My friend Tina was in and out and ready to help however she could. I had all my bases covered as I was going to be with Stoney until the end.

Then things changed. I saw a huge crane coming toward his building and my heart started pounding because I knew this was it. It was late afternoon and security guards were everywhere putting up yellow tape to secure the area. There were several men in suits, the USDA inspector, and lots of commotion. I had my cell phone and the numbers of media newsrooms. I called them all and said I was a tourist and something awful must be happening behind the Luxor Hotel as people were running around and a huge crane had been called. I went outside with my video camera and tried to get some video but was immediately confronted by security and pushed aside and said to get back into the trailer. They had no clue who I was. The tall door rolled open and a huge dumpster with a blue tarp covering it slowly came out and was immediately taken out of sight. I didn't know it at the time, but this was a dumpster with the dead Stoney inside being taken away. Soon after, my friend Tina returned to the trailer and said she heard on the radio that Stoney was dead.

I felt like my insides were on fire and I was falling off a cliff. I can never remember feeling so useless and empty. It was all Tina could do to calm me down at that point. I couldn't believe it. It was unreal. I made the necessary calls to Pat and a few others who tried to help our boy. After a few hours, I went home completely drained and cried out. My husband said the media was trying to get a hold of me for a statement. I wondered where had they been these last few months when so many times I tried to generate a story about Stoney's debilitating condition? Ed Stewart with PAWS gave a statement to the media that I totally stand behind: "We are saddened by Stoney's death and equally saddened by his life." Tina called me and said on her way home she heard on the radio that they buried him at the local pet cemetery. We decided to go there early the next day to see for ourselves.

In a sense, I felt like I had let Stoney down. We were there by seven in the morning and stayed for a couple of hours still in disbelief. Pat had always talked about animals that become "sacrificial lambs" because it takes their suffering to bring attention to what can and does happen to performing animals. I don't remember driving home that morning; I just knew I had to disconnect from everything and everyone. I spent two days in bed with the phone off the hook in a truly dark place. I completely shut down for the first and only time in my life.

Eventually, Pat called my husband at work and asked him to get me on the phone for her. He did, and she talked me back to reality with her loving but stern words of wisdom. *This isn't over*, she told me. She was coming to Las Vegas and we are going to give Stoney a memorial service. I picked her up at the airport and

Afterword

we went to his gravesite. We both knew we had done all we could, yet we felt a heavy sense of failure to our boy. People made wreaths of fruits, vegetables and nuts. A television crew came and told me they were sorry that they didn't do more to try and help. We stayed a couple of hours as close to Stoney as we had even been. Neither Pat nor I ever saw him in person. We only saw him on just a couple of short video clips and some pictures I later was able to dig up. I had a hard time leaving him that day, but I hoped his spirit somehow knew we came to honor him and give him the dignity he never received in the last year of his life.

I go back August 28th every year to visit his grave knowing he isn't there. I bring fruit and vegetables and leave them by his small marker. Even though I couldn't bring them to him when he needed them, doing this somehow makes me feel better. This may seem odd to some, but his story is one that haunts and perseveres. I sit and talk to him and silently shed a few tears and tell him Pat and I will never forget the special being he was. I will close this with what I often say to him at his grave with no one else around. If Stoney were able to hear me, I would tell him:

You are free now, sweet boy, and no one can cause you any more pain. Soar with the eagles, and know you were loved.

-L.F.

Las Vegas, Nevada

Appendix A

Tina and Stoney's Other Siblings

Of Stoney's paternal siblings, the three living elephants include SSP numbers 48, 51, and 52: Packy, Hanako, and Cora (also known as Noel), respectively. Packy is still living at Oregon Zoo. When he was born in 1962, he was the first captive born elephant in the western hemisphere in four decades. Packy's highly publicized birth provided Oregon Zoo much publicity and helped launch their captive elephant breeding program. Packy holds the record for the largest living Asian elephant at 13,500 pounds and a shoulder height of ten feet and six inches. Hanako is a forty-seven-year-old cow currently living at Point Defiance Zoo and Aquarium in Tacoma, Washington, in their Asian Forest Sanctuary. Cora is currently presiding at Two Tails Ranch, a private twenty-acre farm in Williston, Florida.

The remainder of the elephants in this group are dead. Of the twenty-seven elephants born at the Oregon Zoo, ten remain alive as of 2010. Many of them died very young in the sixties, seventies, and early eighties well before the zoo's more progressive species survival program was put in place in 1981 (even though some of these elephants, such as Stoney, were born before the SSP was enacted, they were apparently given SSP numbers after the fact). Me-Tu was euthanized at the Oregon Zoo due to foot ailments at the age of 34. Droopy lived to be three days old and died at the Oregon Zoo from unknown reasons. SSP#56 was not given a name, and the elephant database simply states "Stillborn or killed?" at the Oregon Zoo. SSP#58 was named Judy, and Judy's status and location are presently unknown. Stretch, aka Tuskanini, died at Oregon Zoo at the age of three from unknown reasons. SSP#62 was also not named. He died at three days of white muscle disease, a muscular degeneration and necrosis. SSP#63, Emma, died at the age of thirteen. She went from Oregon Zoo to the San Jose Zoological Gardens to the theme park Busch Gardens in Tampa Bay Florida. This theme park currently houses five living Asian elephants along with many other animals. SSP#59 was named McClane (aka Gabriel) and traveled from the Oregon Zoo to a private elephant trainer in Dangerfield, Texas, and then to the Lincoln Park Zoo in Chicago, Illinois. At the zoo, the only one actually within the city limits of Chicago, elephants lived in an approximately quarter-acre outdoor area and a 3,300-square-foot indoor facility. Lincoln Park Zoo eventually relocated all their elephants. McClane was relocated to a California circus named Circus Vargas and died from an unknown reason at eleven years old. Circus Vargas returned several years ago as an exotic animal-free act. The only animals used in the show presently are small cats and dogs, much more easily cared for than exotics. However, a 2011 attendance of a Circus Vargas performance featured no animals at all. Circus Vargas may well prove to be an example of how a traditional circus can retire their exotic animals and still support the people working for it and depending on it.

Stoney's final paternal sibling is SSP#57, better known as Tina. She proceeded from Oregon Zoo to the Vancouver Game Farm and from there to the African Lion Safari in Cambridge, Ontario. This Canadian facility has made concerted efforts to breed elephants since 1969, and it now has more "second-generation captive births than any other North American institution," according to its Website. With Tina's foot problems worsening, the Canadian Zoo staff decided to retire her to a sanctuary and relocated Tina to the Tennessee Elephant Sanctuary. In a video on the sanctuary's Website, it is stated that the zoo's decision to retire Tina was a statement of their concern and love for her. Tina lived in Tennessee only from August 11, 2003 until July 21, 2004, and became a big hit with the other elephants and the fans of the sanctuary. Her health problems inevitably worsened.

Like many elephants in captivity, Tina had developed severe foot problems and developed what is sometimes called "foot rot," the number one killer of all captive elephants who spend their time standing on concrete, hard-packed dirt, or other unforgiving surfaces. This causes cracks in their skin, and often standing in feces and urine causes infections that can get into the bone. Some elephants have so much necrotic foot tissue removed they lose their entire footpads. The sanctuary has had great success treating this condition, but Tina's was very advanced. The Website of The Elephant Sanctuary (TES) says, "Tina arrived at the Sanctuary with severe chronic pododermatitis and degenerative osteoarthritis. She spent her year with us in hospice care."

Prior to arriving at TES, Tina had not been able to lie down for over a year, which no doubt led to her worsening arthritis. Her joints, which supported her many tons, were bone on bone with no cartilage remaining between them. Upon her death a necropsy was performed, which is standard procedure in the death of most captive elephants. Samples of tissue, bone, and organs were sent to the C.E. Kord Animal Disease Laboratory in Nashville, TN, and the results were retuned on August 9, 2004:

The interventricular septum and left ventricular wall of Tina's heart were approximately 10X the thickness of the right ventricular wall. The right ventricular wall measured approximately 1cm in thickness. No gross lesions were evident in any of the samples; stomach, liver, lung, kidney, pancreas, ovary, spleen or bladder. A nodule on her uterus was identified as a fibrous cyst. Foot lesions consisted of chronic active inflammation. Blood work done prior to her death indicated that Tina's LDH levels were elevated, which could be an indication of a heart problem.

Dr. Steven Scott, Tina's veterinarian of record, concluded that the cause of Tina's death was a heart problem, very possibly a genetic defect. Her death was sudden and shocked the sanctuary staff and her fan club, which followed her progress on TES Website. She was one of the two elephants from this group sired by Thonglaw to make it past the age of thirty, dying at thirty-four.

Appendix B

List of Links to Elephant Investigations, Pictures, and Other Media

The famous picture of Big Mary's hanging can be viewed at the following URL: http://www.blueridgecountry.com/archive/mary-the-elephant.html

A picture of Sport's hanging can be viewed at the following URL: http://www.myspace.com/stoneytheelephant/photos/16154408

The video of Stoney can be viewed at the following URL: http://www.youtube.com/watch?v=f1e_jhFeCxY

A video of Topsy being electrocuted at Coney Park in 1903 can be viewed at the following URL: http://www.youtube.com/watch?v=HMmslGfaNls

Appendix C

List of Every Known Circus and Ride Elephant Accident/Injury from March 26, 1950 to July 1, 2004

This list was compiled by the Performing Animal Welfare Society and can be retrieved from http://www.pawsweb.org/incidents.pdf. Since the list is only current to July 1, 2004, there are many more recent incidents not included. There is no possible way to know every incident, but this list gives an idea of the sheer danger of using elephants in performance situations. In single-spaced twelve point Times New Roman font, the list is over fifty pages long.

Notes

Chapter 1

1. Due to a previously written book on Big Mary (Charles Edwin Price's *The Day They Hung the Elephant*), this book focuses primarily on Stoney's story.

Chapter 2

1. This reported by the Elephant Database. The elephant database is an excellent online resource for anyone attempting to locate information regarding captive elephants. It is found online at www.elephant.se, and the database performs several functions. The number of elephants the database tracks is immense and includes 2,577 dead elephants and 3,012 living elephants in 104 countries as of May 9, 2010. The database, Web-mastered by the professional, friendly, and accessible Dan Koehl in Stockholm, Sweden, makes such tracking distinctions as bulls, cows, wild-caught versus captive born, Asian, African bush and African forest elephants, wild elephants, and elephants living in both exhibiting facilities and nature reserves.
2. Weise, R.J., & Willis, K. (2004, August).
3. Information on Stoney's other siblings is available in Appendix A. In 1989, when they were added to the international list of the most endangered species, there were about 600,000 remaining, less than 1 percent of their original number. Asian elephants were never as abundant as their African cousins, and today they are even more endangered than African elephants. At the turn of the century, there were an estimated 200,000 Asian elephants. Today there are probably no more than 35,000 to 40,000 left in the wild.

http://www.bagheera.com/inthewild/van_anim_elephant.htm
4. Sally helps fill in some of the blanks, as does USDA-APHIS (The United States Department of Agriculture's Animal and Plant Inspection Service) documentation and precious few other sources.

Chapter 3

1. Telephone interview with Sally Joseph.
2. Organizations such as Animal Defenders International, People for the Ethical Treatment of Animals, Mercy for Animals, PAWS, and others have released undercover videos of various aspects of animal abuse including elephants. They are easily found on the Web with simple searches for things such as "elephant training video," "elephant abuse video," and the like.
3. Telephone interview with Pat Derby.

Chapter 4

1. Stoney appears in three issues of *Bandwagon*. That and health reports are the only official sources of these years. Complete information is provided in the bibliography regarding this information.
2. The APHIS arm (Animal and Plant Health Inspection Service) of the USDA oversees the inspection of, among other things, traveling animal exhibitors. It is the overseeing governmental regulatory body charged with the wellbeing and protection of animals used in performance.
3. The February 1992 report continues and cites that Stoney's water trough had a buildup of excess algae, and LaTorres stated the elephant did not drink from it. It was also noted that his habitat contained no shade. At time of the inspection, Stoney was tethered in a pasture, and the inspector found the "animal does not have access to shade or protection from rain while outside of his primary transport enclosure." The

inspector ordered Mike to correct the problem within thirty days. Many of the USDA-APHIS inspection reports resulted in a similar thirty-day period in which to rectify the situation. Many of them were not, and LaTorres simply received further notices with no actual fine or penalty assessed for his noncompliance, as far as I can tell. The actual USDA-APHIS violations occurred in February 27, 1992; January (unknown date), 1994; March 3, 1994; June 19, 1995; and August 3, 1995

Chapter 5

1. The majority of the source material regarding Stoney's final year of life in Las Vegas comes from firsthand accounts, veterinary reports, USDA inspection reports, federal court records (all obtained through Freedom of Information Act requests), communiqués between activists, animal welfare organizations, USDA officials, and the Luxor Hotel (also largely through FOIA requests). Many of the people most closely connected with the case have been interviewed, and all of the above-mentioned sources have contributed insight to his story.
2. Reported by Sally Joseph via phone interview.

Chapter 6

1. This documentation includes detailed notes from multiple veterinarians and the hotel staff.
2. Veterinary incident report dated 4-12-95
3. Pat Derby, Ed Stewart, Cynthia Moss, and Carol Buckley have all publically written about the influence of the bullhook on elephants.
4. Email interview with Ottavio Gesmundo

Chapter 7

1. Vidya, T. & Sukumar, R., 2005

2. *Ibid*, pg.1201
3. Other elephant facilities exist, but PAWS and the Tennessee Elephant Sanctuary are among the leaders.
4. Some of which are dated on October 10, 11, 28, November 21. There are others.
5. Exact measurements are impossible since the shed has since been torn down.
6. Dimensions provided by Dr. Tom Hartgrove's diagrams submitted in evidence during the federal court case that was eventually filed against Mike LaTorres.
7. Average dimension information provided by the Denver Zoo. www.denverzoo.org/downloads/dzoo_asian_elephant.pdf
8. Dr. Martin Dinnes

Chapter 8

1. An employee supplied Linda Faso with a copy of the minutes.
2. A USDA-APHIS inspection report dated June 19, 1995
3. Derby and PAWS were vehemently against Stoney's being transferred to the Arkansas facility. It should be noted, however, that other people had no problem with the facility.
4. Interview with Dr. Tom Hartgrove conducted by M. Jaynes
5. The veterinary notes, letters, and inspection reports in this chapter were all obtained through Freedom of Information Act public record requests and are cited in the bibliography.

Chapter 9

1. Information is in his September 13th, 1995, letter written after Stoney's death.
2. On August 17, 1995, Dr. Dinnes wrote a letter to Dr. V. Wensley Koch, the Western Sector Supervisor of the USDA/APHIS/REAL detailing plans of Stoney's relocation.
3. Csuti, B., & Sargent, E. L., and Bechert, S.U. (2001). The

Notes

Elephant's Foot: Prevention and Care of Foot Conditions in Captive Asian and African Elephants, pg. 3.
4. Telephone interview with Dr. Elliot Katz of In Defense of Animals.
5. Csuti, B. *et al.*, p. 5
6. *Ibid.* p. 81
7. *Ibid.* p. 53
8. *Ibid.* p. 53
9. *Ibid.* p. 53
10. *Ibid.* p. 54
11. *Ibid.* p. 54
12. *Ibid.* p. 54
13. *Ibid.* p. 54
14. The TAOS has been replaced by the Global Federation of Animal Sanctuaries (GFAS). TES belongs to it as does PAWS.
15. According to Linda Faso.

Chapter 11

1. This reeks of the age-old hasty generalization regarding all show people. As mentioned, I was guilty of this same generalization in my early writings on this particular subject as well and have apologized where applicable. In fact, this book supersedes all writing I have previously published on animal performance. Prior to researching this book, I held a less nuanced and informed opinion on the subject of animal performance. I now understand the truth is usually much more complex than it initially appears. Regarding the comment about the trainer, it is unlikely that the reporter did extensive research into LaTorres. I have, and I think the comment is unfair and inaccurate.
2. It is true many zoos are truly conservation-minded regarding elephants. For example, PAWS sings the praises of the Oakland Zoo, The Detroit Zoo, and several others. Not all zoos are "bad," say Pat and Ed.

3. Chang Dee, also called Prince, has been retired to PAWS.

Chapter 12

1. Csuti, B. *et al.*, p. 3

Chapter 13

1. See his section in the epilogue for more reasoning behind this statement.
2. Email interview with Dr. Cynthia Moss.
3. Email interview with Debbie Leahy.
4. According to Linda Faso.

PART II

1. In fact, much of this chapter is updated and adapted from a previously published article I wrote, "The hanging of Big Mary: someone worth remembering," published by the Captive Animals Protection Society in 2008.
2. Charles Edwin Price's *The Day they Hung the Elephant*. Price's book (which is oft quoted and paraphrased in this part of the book) is, to date, the only in-depth study of Big Mary's story. The slim volume is partially supposition, but it is required reading for anyone intrigued with Big Mary In the early nineties, Price spent two years in Johnson City, TN; Erwin, TN; and St. Paul, VA, and the surrounding area interviewing the few remaining surviving witnesses to the hanging. He also compiled material from listening to oral history tapes from the Archives of Appalachia at East Tennessee State University. In fact, ETSU now houses his work, and the Price papers contain the most research gathered in one place regarding Mary. An Appalachian native, Price was born in 1941 and has specialized as a freelance writer in Southern Appalachian folklore, ghost lore, and local history. A graduate of East Tennessee State University, Price has taught writing seminars, produced folklore segments for National Public Radio's "All Things Considered" and documentaries.

He is the author of several books, including *Haints, Witches and Boogers: Tales from Upper East Tennessee* (1992), *The Day They Hung the Elephant* (1992), and *The Infamous Bell Witch of Tennessee* (1993). More info about the collection can be found on ETSU's Website. This project is very grateful to have the benefit of his research on Big Mary and *The Day they Hung the Elephant*.

3. Price, C. p. 4
4. Burton, T. pg. 1
5. Price, C. p. 10
6. Burton, T. p. 2
7. Burton, T. p. 2; Price, C. p. 10
8. Burton, T. p. 1
9. Thomas Edison videotaped the execution and later released it under the name "Electrocuting an Elephant." The video can be viewed at http://www.youtube.com/watch?v=HMmslGfaNls For an intriguing account of the life of Topsy, please see Chapter 15 ("Topsy Was Framed") in Eric Scigliano's Love, War, and Circuses.
10. Dominey, C.
11. The URL of a photo of Sport's hanging is included in appendix B.
12. Burton, T. p. 1
13. Padgett, H.
14. Mary (Big Mary, Murderous Mary) at Sparks Circus. The Elephant Database. http://www.elephant.se/database2.php?elephant_id=1974 Accessed on 12-15-08]
15. Email interview with Steve Shelton.
16. Price, C. p. 16
17. Vannorsdall, S.
18. Burton, T. p. 7
19. Burton, T. p. 6
20. Dominey, C.
21. Big Mary's entry on Dan Koehl's Elephant Database.

22. In his book, Price credits the photo to LeSeurer. Burton's article discusses other sources of the photo.
23. Burton, T. p. 6
24. Vincent, p. 147 qtd in Burton, T. p. 6
25. Burton, T. p. 5
26. Burton, T. p. 7
27. Burton, T. p. 5
28. All the following versions are adapted from the previously cited Joan Vannorsdall Schroeder's article, "There's a Skeleton in a Train Yard in East Tennessee," and Thomas Burton's 1971 article.
29. Bradshaw, G. et al.
30. Brown, A.
31. Vannorsdall-Schroder, J.
32. I have seen Ruth Piper's last name spelled both "Piper" and "Pieper," as in this article. As attempts to contact her were unsuccessful, I am unsure as to the correct spelling and apologize for any inaccuracy.
33. Plous, S. p. 509
34. Scigliano, E. p. 203
35. Price, C. p. 3
36. Price, C. p. 39
37. James, L.
38. Price, C. Cover illustration.
39. Amboseli Trust for Elephants' statement on the use of elephants in circuses. http://www.elephanttrust.org/node/414.

Epilogue

1. Information provided by Sally Joseph.

Bibliography

ADI Press Release on Chipperfield Circus' going animal-free. (2010, October 21). Tim Phillips of Animal Defenders International speaks about the once-infamous circus becoming a human-only show. www.ad-international.org.

Amboseli Trust for Elephants' statement on the use of elephants in circuses. http://www.elephanttrust.org/node/414.

Animal Care Inspection Report. (1992, February 27). U.S. Department of Agriculture: Animal and Plant Health Inspection Service. APHIS forms 7008 prepared by illegible. Received by James M. LaTorres.

—. (1995, June 19). U.S. Department of Agriculture: Animal and Plant Health Inspection Service. APHIS forms 7008 prepared by Greg Wallen. Received by James M. LaTorres.

—. (1995, August 3). U.S. Department of Agriculture: Animal and Plant Health Inspection Service. APHIS forms 7100 prepared by Greg Wallen. Received by James M. LaTorres.

—. (1995, August 10). U.S. Department of Agriculture: Animal and Plant Health Inspection Service. APHIS forms 7100 prepared by Greg Wallen. Received by James M. LaTorres.

Average dimensions of adult Asian elephants. www.denverzoo.org/downloads/dzoo_asian_elephant.pdf

Blais, S. & Buckley, C. (2008, July 24) "'They're like us,' elephant researchers say

Body of trainer recovered from guard of bull elephant. (1979, June 28). *Eugene Register-Guard*. Retrieved from http://news.google.com/newspapers?nid=1310&dat=19790628&id=uXAR AAAAIBAJ&sjid=MeIDAAAAIBAJ&pg=6586,8818440

Bradshaw, G., Schore, A., Brown, J., Poole, J., Moss, C. (2005, February 24). Elephant breakdown: Social trauma: early disruption of attachment can affect physiology, behavior and culture of animals and humans over generations. *Nature*, 433 807.

Brown, A. K. 1916 Elephant hanging still haunts Erwin, TN Retrieved from: http://digg.com/world_news/1916_Elephant _Hanging_Still_Haunts_Erwin_TN

Brummette, J. (2011). "Trains, chains, blame, and elephant appeal: a case study of the public relations significance of Mary the elephant." *Public Relations Review* December 26.

Burton, T. (1971) "The Hanging of Mary, A Circus Elephant." Tennessee Folklore Society Bulletin. 37(1), pp. 1–8.

Chamaille-Jammes, S. & Valeix, M. & Fritz. (2007). "Managing Heterogeneity in Elephant Distribution: Interactions between Elephant Population Density and Surface Water Availability." *Centre d Etudes Biologiques de Chize. Integrated Wildlife Management Research Unit.* Campus Internationale de Baillarguet. Montpellier, France. Retrieved from http://onlinelibrary.wiley.com/doi/10.1111/j.1365-2664.2007.01300.x/abstract

Chambers, P. (2009). *Jumbo: this being the true story of the greatest elephant in the world.* Hanover: Steerforth Press.

Conference for the International Trade in Endangered Species of Wild Fauna and Flora (CITES) Final decisions on the proposals for amendment of Appendices I and II. (2010, April 30). Fifteenth meeting of the Conference of the Parties Doha (Qatar), 13–25 March 2010. Retrieved from http://www.cites.org/eng/cop/15/prop/results.shtml

Crushing by Elephant. Entry in the *New World Encyclopedia*. Retrieved from http://www.newworldencyclopedia.org/entry/Crushing_by_elephant accessed in 2011

Csuti, B., & Sargent, E. L., & Bechert, S.U. (2001). *The elephant's foot: Prevention and care of foot conditions in captive Asian and African elephants.* Ames: Iowa State University Press.

Darren, W. (2009). The elephant, the photographer, and the

sheriff. *Cowlitz County Law Enforcement History.* [Web Log Post] Retrieved from http://cclehistory.blogspot.com/2009/10/elephant-photographer-and-sheriff.html.

Delaney, J. (1998, April 2). Pet Cemetery. *Las Vegas Sun.* 1c.

Derby, P. (1996). Letter to Mike Sloan, Vice President and General Counsel, Circus Circus Enterprises.

—. (1995, August 29). Stoney the Elephant Dies in Las Vegas. Press release of the Performing Animal Welfare Society, P.O. Box 849, Galt, CA, 95632.

—. (1995, August 29). Stoney the Elephant is dead: Luxor hotel's hidden elephant finally succumbs. Press release of the Performing Animal Welfare Society, P.O. Box 849, Galt, CA, 95632.

—. (1995, August 25). Secrets of the Luxor Pyramid-the mystery of the hidden elephant. Press release of the Performing Animal Welfare Society, P.O. Box 849, Galt, CA, 95632.

—. (1995, July 17). Director of the Performing Animal Welfare Society, P.O. Box 849, Galt, CA, 95632 and Linda Faso: Letter correspondence to Dr. Ron De Haven, USDA, 9850 Micron Avenue Suite J, Sacramento, CA, 95827.

—. (1995, July 17). Director of the Performing Animal Welfare Society, P.O. Box 849, Galt, CA, 95632. Letter correspondence to Dr. Ron De Haven, USDA, 9850 Micron Avenue Suite J, Sacramento, CA, 95827.

—. (1995, August 26). Director of the Performing Animal Welfare Society, P.O. Box 849, Galt, CA, 95632. Letter correspondence to Mr. Terry Winnick, Circus Circus Enterprise, 2880 Las Vegas Blvd South, Las Vegas, NV, 89109.

—. (2007–2010) Several email and telephone interviews conducted by M. Jaynes.

—. (2005, August 25). Director of the Performing Animal Welfare Society, P.O. Box 849, Galt, CA, 95632. Letter correspondence to Dr. Dale F. Schwindaman.

Dinnes, M. (1995, August 17). Letter correspondence to Dr. Virginia Wensley Koch, Western Sector Supervisor, USDA/APHIS/REAL. re: Stoney the Elephant. Retrieved through the United States Freedom of Information Act as Government exhibit 9E in the United States Department of Agriculture trial against James Michael LaTorres. 4 pages. AWA Docket No. 96-56. APHIS form 7070.

—. (1995, September 13). Letter correspondence to Mr. J. David Neal, Senior Investigator, USDA/APHIS/REAL. Retrieved through the United States Freedom of Information Act as Government exhibit 8E in the United States Department of Agriculture trial against James Michael LaTorres. AWA Docket No. 96-56. APHIS form 7070.

Dominey, C. (2008). Murderous Mary. Retrieved from http://themoonlitroad.com/murderous-mary

Doughton, S. (2010, March 12). Scientists seek moratorium on ivory to protect elephants. *Chattanooga News Free Press.* C6.

Douglas-Hamilton, I. & Douglas-Hamilton, O. (1975). *Among the elephants.* New York: Viking.

—. (1992). *Battle for the elephants.* New York: Viking.

Ebrey, P., Walthall, A., & Palais, J. (2006). *East Asia: A cultural, social, and political history.* Boston: Houghton Mifflin Company.

Elephant Intelligence in *Wikipedia.* Retrieved from http://en.wikipedia.org/wiki/Elephant_intelligence#Death_ritual

Elephant Protection Project. (1999). *Captive Animals' Protection Society.* Retrieved from http://www.captiveanimals.org/elephants/epp.htm

Elephant put to death: Hanged on a mammoth freight derrick. (1900, June 8). *The New York Times.* Retrieved from http://query.nytimes.com/mem/archive-free/pdf?res=F70E16F6345811738DDDA10894DE405B808CF1D3

Elephants in Musth. (2006). Retrieved from http://www.solarnavigator.net/animal_kingdom/mammals/elephants.htm

Epstein, R. (1993, August 24) Circus life drives animals insane, two British rights groups contend. Associated Press. Retrieved from http://www.dartt-online.org/entertainment.html

Factsheet. (2008). Surplus animals the cycle of hell: a study of captive wildlife in the United States. *Performing Animal Welfare Society*. Retrieved from www.pawsweb.org/surplus.pdf

Factsheet. (2010, July 12). Remaining population of the blue whale. New York State Department of Environmental Conservation. Retrieved from http://www.dec.ny.gov/animals/9367.html

Factsheet. Circus and ride elephant incidents. (2004). *Performing Animal Welfare Society* Retrieved from http://www.pawsweb.org/incidents.pdf

Factsheet: (2010). Ten facts about animals in zoos. *Captive Animals Protection Society* Retrieved from http://www.captiveanimals.org/zoos/zfact1.htm

Factsheet: http://www.circuses.com/pdfs/RinglingElephantBreedingFS.pdf

Factsheet: The crusade by animal special interest groups to remove elephants from circuseshttp://www.ringlingbrostrialinfo.com/uploadedFiles/Special%20Interest%20Groups%20P ending%20Legislation%20F.pdf 2-16-10 Feld Entertainment. www.ringlingbrotherstrialinfo.com 2-16-10

Faso, L. (1996, September 1). Stoney's death good time to remember animal abuse. Letter to the Editor. *Las Vegas Sun*.

—. (1995, July 10). A vigil for Stoney the forgotten elephant at the Luxor hotel. Activism press release.

—. (2007–2010) Several email and telephone interviews conducted by M. Jaynes.

Fagles, R. Trans. (2008). *Aeneid*. New York: Penguin Classics.

Florida Department of Agriculture and Consumer Services Health Certificate for Movement of Zoo Animals. (1985, April 22). Stoney the elephant owned by James Michael LaTorres,

5730 Russo Road, Bartow, FL, 33830. . Examined for: traveling show in Lakespur, CO. Examined by: Thomas B. Schotman, DVM.

—. (1984, May 11). Stoney the elephant owned by James Michael LaTorres, 5730 Russo Road, Bartow, FL, 33830. . Examined for: Shriner Temple, Wilmington, DE. Examined by: Thomas B. Schotman, DVM.

—. (1987, January 14). Stoney the elephant owned by James Michael LaTorres, 5730 Russo Road, Bartow, FL, 33830. . Examined for: local use in Bartow, Florida. Examined by: Thomas B. Schotman, DVM.

—. (1987, May 16). Stoney the elephant owned by James Michael LaTorres, 5730 Russo Road, Bartow, FL, 33830. Examined for: Lake Wells Veterinarian Hospital, Massachusetts. Examined by: Thomas B. Schotman, DVM.

—. (1988, March 12). Stoney the elephant owned by James Michael LaTorres, 5730 Russo Road, Bartow, FL, 33830. Examined for: Shriner Circus, Wilkes-Barre, PA. Examined by: Thomas B. Schotman, DVM.

—. (1988, June 30). Stoney the elephant owned by James Michael LaTorres, 5730 Russo Road, Bartow, FL, 33830. Examined for: Briston Renaissance Fair, Kenosha, WI. Examined by: Thomas B. Schotman, DVM.

—. (1989, March 28). Stoney the elephant owned by James Michael LaTorres, 5730 Russo Road, Bartow, FL, 33830. Examined for: Shriner Circus, Grand Rapids, MI and Indianapolis, IN. Examined by: Thomas B. Schotman, DVM.

—. (1990, March 19). Stoney the elephant owned by James Michael LaTorres, 5730 Russo Road, Bartow, FL, 33830. Examined for: Tommy Hanneford Circus, various stops including: Greenwood, SC; Greenville, SC; Dallas, TX; Houston, TX; Sulfur Springs, TX; Little Rock, AK; and Tampa, Fl. Examined by: Thomas B. Schotman, DVM.

—. (1990, February 9). Stoney the elephant owned by James

Michael LaTorres, 5730 Russo Road, Bartow, FL, 33830. Examined for: multiple stops in Kansas, Missouri, Arkansas, and Illinois. Examined by: Thomas B. Schotman, DVM.

—. (1991, January 4). Stoney the elephant owned by James Michael LaTorres, 5730 Russo Road, Bartow, FL, 33830. Examined for: Shriner Circus, Flint, MI. Examined by: Thomas B. Schotman, DVM.

—. (1991, April 7). Stoney the elephant owned by James Michael LaTorres, 5730 Russo Road, Bartow, FL, 33830. Examined for: Shriner Circus Road Show, Houston, TX; Dayton, OH; Cincinnati, OH. Examined by: Thomas B. Schotman, DVM.

—. (1991, September 20). Stoney the elephant owned by James Michael LaTorres, 5730 Russo Road, Bartow, FL, 33830. Examined for: Shriner Circus, Warrensville Heights, OH. Examined by: Thomas B. Schotman, DVM.

—. (1991, May 12)). Stoney the elephant owned by James Michael LaTorres, 5730 Russo Road, Bartow, FL, 33830. Examined for: Jolly Roger Park, Ocean City, NJ. Examined by: Thomas B. Schotman, DVM.

—. (1991, February 20). Stoney the elephant owned by James Michael LaTorres, 5730 Russo Road, Bartow, FL, 33830. Examined for: Royal Hanneford Circus, Davies, FL. Examined by: Thomas B. Schotman, DVM.

—. (1992, March 30). Stoney the elephant owned by James Michael LaTorres, 5730 Russo Road, Bartow, FL, 33830. Examined for: Hanneford Road Show, Flint, MI; and Saganaw, MI. Examined by: Thomas B. Schotman, DVM.

—. (1992, February 19). Stoney the elephant owned by James Michael LaTorres, 5730 Russo Road, Bartow, FL, 33830. Examined for: Greenwood Civic Center, Greenwood, SC. Examined by: Thomas B. Schotman, DVM.

—. (1992, March 11). Stoney the elephant owned by James Michael LaTorres, 5730 Russo Road, Bartow, FL, 33830.

Examined for: Various locations, Bartow, FL. Examined by: Thomas B. Schotman, DVM.

—. (1993, February). Stoney the elephant owned by James Michael LaTorres, 5730 Russo Road, Bartow, FL, 33830. Examined for: Road Show with Various Stops. Examined by: Thomas B. Schotman, DVM.

—. (1993, March). Stoney the elephant owned by James Michael LaTorres, 5730 Russo Road, Bartow, FL, 33830. Examined for: Road Show with Various Stops. Examined by: Thomas B. Schotman, DVM.

—. Certificate for temporary entrance into Canada. (1993, April 14). VS form 17-140. Stoney the elephant owned by James Michael LaTorres, 5730 Russo Road, Bartow, FL, 33830. Examined for: Cirque Universal, Cowansville, Quebec. Examined by: Thomas B. Schotman, DVM.

Fox, R. *Alexander the Great*. New York: Penguin. 2004

Francione, G. (2008). *Animals as persons: Essays on the abolition of animal exploitation*. Columbia: Columbia University Press.

Gale, J. G. (1995, September 4). Where was USDA before elephant died? *Las Vegas Sun*. 10b.

Gesmundo, O. (2010). Email interview conducted by M. Jaynes.

Gipson, C. (2010, September 1). Deputy Administrator for Animal Care, APHIS. APHIS Animal Care creates team to inspect traveling elephant exhibitors. Provided by Donald W. Elroy, Director of Captive Wildlife Advocacy Stop Animal Exploitation Now! (SAEN)

Glotzbach, C. (1977). Souvenir program and coloring book of the International All-Star Circus. Nordmark & Hood Presentations, Inc. Circus Plaza Building, 1770 Wood Street, Sarasota, FL, 33577. 4 pages.

Graef, A. Stop the Slaughter of Elephants for Ivory. Website of *In Defense of Animals*. Retrieved from http://idausa.org/

Graves, E., ed. (1976). *Elephants & other land giants*. New York: Time Life Films and Vineyard Books, Inc.

Greene, S. (1995, August 29). Luxor elephant Stoney dies following leg injury. *Las Vegas Review-Journal.*
Griffith, L. (2008, April 25) Circus elephants and tuberculosis. [Web Log Post]. Retrieved from: http://www.lesliegriffithproductions.com/my_weblog/2008/04/circus-elephant.html
—. (2008, April 25). Circus elephants and tuberculosis. [Web Log Post]. Retrieved from http://www.lesliegriffithproductions.com/my_weblog/2008/04/circus-elephant.html
Hartgrove, T. (1994, October 11). Veterinary Prescription for Stoney the elephant from the practice of Equine Veterinarian Tom Hartgrove, DVM. 7375 Rome Blvd. Las Vegas, Nevada 89131. Retrieved through the United States Freedom of Information Act as Government exhibit 8E in the United States Department of Agriculture trial against James Michael LaTorres. AWA Docket No. 96-56. Page 39 of 45, APHIS form 7070.
—. (1994, October 1). Veterinary Prescription for Stoney the elephant from the practice of Equine Veterinarian Tom Hartgrove, DVM. 7375 Rome Blvd. Las Vegas, Nevada 89131. Retrieved through the United States Freedom of Information Act as Government exhibit 8E in the United States Department of Agriculture trial against James Michael LaTorres. AWA Docket No. 96-56. Page 35 of 45, APHIS form 7070.
—. (1994, October 28). Veterinary notes for Stoney the elephant from the practice of Equine Veterinarian Tom Hartgrove, DVM. 7375 Rome Blvd. Las Vegas, Nevada 89131. Retrieved through the United States Freedom of Information Act as Government exhibit 8E in the United States Department of Agriculture trial against James Michael LaTorres. AWA Docket No. 96-56. Page 34 of 45, APHIS form 7070.
—. (1994, November 21). Veterinary notes and prescription for Stoney the elephant from the practice of Equine

Veterinarian Tom Hartgrove, DVM. 7375 Rome Blvd. Las Vegas, Nevada 89131. Retrieved through the United States Freedom of Information Act as Government exhibit 8E in the United States Department of Agriculture trial against James Michael LaTorres. AWA Docket No. 96-56. Page 28 of 45, APHIS form 7070.

—. (1995, April 3). Veterinary notes for Stoney the elephant from the practice of Equine Veterinarian Tom Hartgrove, DVM. 7375 Rome Blvd. Las Vegas, Nevada 89131. Retrieved through the United States Freedom of Information Act as Government exhibit 8F in the United States Department of Agriculture trial against James Michael LaTorres. AWA Docket No. 96-56. Page 2 of 3, APHIS form 7070.

—. (1995, April 12). Veterinary notes for Stoney the elephant from the practice of Equine Veterinarian Tom Hartgrove, DVM. 7375 Rome Blvd. Las Vegas, Nevada 89131.

—. (1994, October 28). Veterinary notes for Stoney the elephant from the practice of Equine Veterinarian Tom Hartgrove, DVM. 7375 Rome Blvd. Las Vegas, Nevada 89131. Diagram of crush revealing its physical parameters

—. (1994, September 7). Sworn Affidavit. Equine Veterinarian Tom Hartgrove, DVM. 7375 Rome Blvd. Las Vegas, Nevada 89131. Retrieved through the United States Freedom of Information Act as Government exhibit 8F in the United States Department of Agriculture trial against James Michael LaTorres. AWA Docket No. 96-56. Page 3 of 3.

Henderson, Mark. (2007, February 27). 23,000 elephants killed each year for ivory. *The Sunday Times*. Retrieved from http://www.timesonline.co.uk/tol/news/science/article1443967.ece

Herrmann, A. (2005, January 15). Second Lincoln park zoo elephant, Peaches, dies. *Chicago Sun Times*. Retrieved from http://www.elephants.com/news/globalnews.php?newsSubCategory_id=11#392

Hershaft, A. (2008, winter). The siren song of welfare reforms. *The Animals Voice Magazine* 16.

Hile, J. (2002, October 16). Activists denounce Thailand's elephant "crushing" ritual *National Geographic Today* Retrieved from http://news.nationalgeographic.com /news/ 2002/10/1016_021016_phajaan.html.

Honolulu Star Bulletin. Carol Buckley and Jim Rogers quotes. Retrieved from archives.starbulletin.com/2004/08/16/news/ story2.html

Incident Report. (1994, September 23). Luxor Hotel and Casino. 3900 S. Las Vegas Blvd. Las Vegas, Nevada, 89119. Report #LX94-09-007646. Provided by Linda Faso

Irwin, P. (2000). *Losing paradise: the growing threat to our animals, our environment, and ourselves.* New York: Square One Publishers.

James, L. (2008). It's hard to kill an elephant. [Web Log Post]. Retrieved from http://laurajames.typepad.com/clews/2006/07 /its_hard_to_kil.html

Jensen, J. (2009, April 3). Elephant car wash at wildlife safari Oregon wild animal park adds fun tourist attraction *Suite 101.com* Retrieved from http://oregontravel.suite101.com/ article.cfm/ elephant_car_wash_at_wildlife_safari

Jobaria and the Elephant. *Project Exploration.* Retrieved from http://www.projectexploration.org/jobaria/Rearing2.html

Joseph, S. (2010). Series of email and phone interviews conducted in April, May, and June of 2010.

Katz, E. (2010) Email interview conducted by M. Jaynes.

Kistler, J.M. (2007) *War Elephants.* Westport: Praeger.

—. (2009, April 9). I-Team: Animal activists hope lawsuit protects circus elephants. Retrieved from http://www. 8newsnow.com/Global/story.asp?s=10160295&.

Koch, V. W. (1995, August 24) Letter correspondence to Martin R. Dinnes, Dinnes Memorial Veterinary Hospital, 9316 Soledad Canyon Road, Santa Clarita, CA 91350. Retrieved through the

United States Freedom of Information Act as Government exhibit 9D in the United States Department of Agriculture trial against James Michael LaTorres. AWA Docket No. 96-56. APHIS form 7070.

Lalchandani, N. & Chopra, D. (2009, November 12). "Elephants to be banished from all zoos." *The Times of India* Retrieved from http://timesofindia.indiatimes.com/home/environment/flora-fauna/Elephants-to-be-banished-from-all-zoos/articleshow/5221159.cms

Lofton, J.M. & Cashill, R. (1998, October 1). Pyramid power: Relamping—-and revamping—-the Luxor in Las Vegas with new venues." Retrieved from http://livedesignonline.com/mag/lighting_pyramid_power_relampingand/

Luxor Hotel and Casino. (1995, March 23). Staff meeting minutes. Memo number 15. Provided by Linda Faso.

Mackenzie, Paul. (2001). Elephant evolution. *Elephant Information Repository.* Retrieved from http://elephant.elehost.com/About_Elephants/Stories/Evolution/evolution.html

Mary (Big Mary, Murderous Mary) at Sparks Circus (2008). in *The Elephant Database.* Retrieved from http://www.elephant.se/database2.php?elephant_id=1974.

McComb, K., Baker, L., & Moss, C. (2005, October 25) African Elephants show high Levels of Interest in the Skulls and Ivory of their own Species. *Biology Letters, 2*(2). 26–28.

Metz Epitome. 54. Retrieved from http://www.ncbi.nlm.nih.gov/pmc/articles/PMC1617198/

Miller, R. (2005, February 17). Ancient elephants. Retrieved from http://www.greenwichtime.com/news/article/Ancient-elephants-106931.

Moss, C. (2010) Email interview conducted by M. Jaynes.

Mundy, P. (2006, October). The African Elephant—Something to Cherish and to Use. *International Journal of Environmental Studies, 63* (5). 587–597. Retrieved from http://www.informaworld.com/smpp/content~db=all~content=a758723561

Bibliography

Ned's Bio. Elephants.com Official website of the Tennessee Elephant Sanctuary. Retrieved from http://www.elephants.com/Ned/ned_bio.htm

Nocella II, A. J. (2005). The game is over: Taking the A.L.F. seriously. Ed. Richard Kahn. *Animal Liberation Front.com: Worldwide News and Information Source About the A.L.F.* Retrieved from: http://www.animalliberationfront.com/Philosophy/TheGameIsOver.htm

Nowotny, R. A. (2008). Mary the elephant. [Web Log Post]. Retrieved from http://needtovent movies.blogspot.com/2007/03/mary-elephant.html

Oesterle, J. & Crindland, T. (2007). *Weird Las Vegas and Nevada.* New York: Sterling Publishing Co.

Padgett, Hilda. "The Hanging of Mary the Elephant" http://www.rootsweb.ancestry.com/~tnunicoi/mary.htm Accessed on 12-15-08]

Payne, K. & Douglas-Hamilton, I. (2002, October 31). Lifting the ivory ban called premature: Scientists offer a perspective on elephants and ivory. Retrieved from http://www.npr.org/templates/story/story.php?storyId=3879214

Peace. ABC News. Retrieved from http://abcnews.go.com/Health/Story?id=5435466&page=4.

Pfening, III., F. D. (1990, January-February). 1989 Season: the Circus Year in Review. *Bandwagon: The Journal of the Circus Historical Society.* 34(1). Pg. 12.

—. (1991, January-February).The Circus Year in Review: 1990 Season. *Bandwagon: The Journal of the Circus Historical Society.* 35(1). Pg. 10 and 43.

—. (1994, January-February). The Circus Year in Review: 1993 Season. *Bandwagon: The Journal of the Circus Historical Society.* 38(1). Pg. 13

Phuangkum, P., Lair, R.C., & Angkawanith, T. (2005). *Elephant care manual for mahouts and camp managers* Series title: RAP Publication.169 pg. Retrieved from http://www.cabdirect

.org/abstracts/20063083638.html?start=550

Please say no because animals can't. (2008, June 30). In *Circuses.com*. Retrieved June 30, 2008, from http://www.circuses.com

Plotnick, J., de Waal, F., & Reiss, D. (2006, September 13). Self-recognition in an Asian Elephant. *PNAS, 103*(45). 17053-17057. Retrieved from http://www.ncbi.nlm.nih.gov/pmc/articles/PMC1636577/

Plous, S. (2002). Is there such a thing as prejudice toward animals? in *Understanding Prejudice and Discrimination*. New York: McGraw Hill Humanities.

Poole, J. (2010) Email interview conducted by M. Jaynes.

Price, C. E. (1992). *The day they hung the elephant*. Johnson City: The Overmountain Press.

Quintus Curtius Rufus (60–70 AD). Historiae Alexandri Magni. 8.13.6. As quoted in http://en.academic.ru/dic.nsf/enwiki/378337

Rajaran, A. (2006). Biophysics and Electron Microscopy Laboratory, Central Leather Research Instutiue, Adyar Chaennai, India. "Musth in Elephants" *Resonance*. October 2006.

Ralston, S. (1995, September 17). Hotel was not responsible for the tragedy of Stoney. *Las Vegas Sun*. Sunday edition.

—. (1995, October 27). Corporate Director of Public Relations, Circus Circus Enterprises, Inc. Letter correspondence to Mrs. Linda Faso.

Rider, T. (2000, June 13). Official testimony of Tom Rider, legislative hearing on H.R.2929. Retrieved from http://judiciary.house.gov/legacy/crime.htm

Ross, D.H. (1992, October). Elephant: The animal and its ivory in African Culture. *African Arts, 25*(4) 65–108

Schiller, C.A. (1994, October 11). Veterinary Pathology Laboratory Results. APE Veterinary Laboratories. Retrieved through the United States Freedom of Information Act as

Government exhibit 8E in the United States Department of Agriculture trial against James Michael LaTorres. AWA Docket No. 96-56. Page 37 of 45, APHIS form 7070.

Schmidt, M. (1994, September 26). Veterinary notes. Retrieved through the United States Freedom of Information Act as Government exhibit 8E in the United States Department of Agriculture trial against James Michael LaTorres. AWA Docket No. 96-56. Page 2 of 45, APHIS form 7070.

—. (1995, September 15). Veterinary consultation for LUXOR Casino concerning the elephant "Stoney." Retrieved through the United States Freedom of Information Act as Government exhibit 8E in the United States Department of Agriculture trial against James Michael LaTorres. AWA Docket No. 96-56. APHIS form 7070.

Schulberg, P. (1996, November 21). KATU's elephant story rattles cages at Washington Park Zoo. *The Oregonian.* E7.

Scigliano, E. (2002). *Love, war, and circuses: The age-old relationship between elephants and humans.* New York: Houghton Mifflin.

Scott, C. (1995, August 29). Luxor show elephant found dead. *Las Vegas Sun.*

Scully, M. (2002). *Dominion: The suffering of animals, the power of man, and the call to mercy.* New York: St. Martin's Press.

Shemeligian, B. (1995, July 11). Group protests fate of injured elephant. *Las Vegas Sun.* 1a-4a.

Sloan, M. H. (1995). Vice President and General Counsel of Circus Circus Enterprises, Inc. Letter correspondence to Mr. Lonnie King, Administrator of APHIS. Provided by Linda Faso.

Smithsonian National Zoo. People–Elephant Conflict: Monitoring how Elephants Use Agricultural Crops in Sri Lanka. (2008, February 29) *Smithsonian National Zoological Park Review.* Retrieved from http://nationalzoo.si.edu/scbi/ConservationGIS/projects/asian_elephants/conflict.cfm

Steiner, G. (2005). *Anthropocentrism and its discontents: the moral status of animals in the history of western philosophy*. Pittsburgh: University of Pittsburgh Press.

Stoddard, E. (2005, October 4). CITES lifts ban on hunting black rhino. Retrieved from http://www.planetark.com/dailynews story.cfm/newsid/27518/story.htm

Topsy (elephant) in *Wikipedia*. Retrieved from http://en.wikipedia.org/wiki/Topsy_(elephant)

United States Department of Agriculture before the Secretary of Agriculture. (1996, June 6). Trial notes of the USDA APHIS vs. James Michael LaTorres. AWA Docket number 96-56. Retrieved through the United States Freedom of Information Act. Prepared by Frank Martin, Jr. Attorney for Complainant. Office of the General Counsel, USDA, Washington D.C., 20250-1400.

—. (1996, June 6). Trial notes, Explanation of evidence proving violation, other evidence, exhibit list, and witness list of the USDA APHIS vs. James Michael LaTorres. AWA Docket number 96-56. Retrieved through the United States Freedom of Information Act.

—. (1997, July 28). Final result of the USDA APHIS vs. James Michael LaTorres, decision and order. AWA Docket number 97-0012. Retrieved through the United States Freedom of Information Act.

U.S. continues to demonstrate leadership on elephant conservation. (2010). *U.S. CITES.gov*. Retrieved from http://www.uscites.gov/update/us-continues-demonstrate-leadership-elephant-conservation.

Van Aarde, R. Elephant population biology and ecology. Retrieved from http://docs.google.com/viewer?a=v&q=cache :ke4yILQ35noJ:www.elephantassessment.co.za/files/04_ch2_E lephant%2520Management.pdf+is+elephant+reproduction+ke yed+to+water+availability&hl=en&gl=us&pid=bl&srcid=ADG EESjiF8kFslc7nBF2VaFTyH-XvxaTGMrPHB7ViW-MJwSsEo_iP7qfT9mHo5NledoY1nlcqrCX1tsLoag4s1tG8Ke-

3zYFLlDe0JSpW7CZhjiFAii83xJBVSzyWeNCHs9aO9nEnX8U
&sig=AHIEtbSKfRP5CNTggnG0QOWl7E-7MEEjNg

Vannorsdall S. J. (1993). There's a skeleton in a train yard in east Tennessee. Retrieved from: http://www.blueridgecountry.com/elephant/elephant.htm 1

Video of Stoney performing, restrained in his crush, and vocalizing while attempting to rise to his feet on August 28, 1995. Retrieved from http://www.youtube.com/watch?v=Sc5T5dNz MF8

Vidya, T., Sukumar, R. (2005, October). Social and Reproductive Behavior in Elephants. *Current Science, 89*(7). 1200–1207. Retrieved from http://www.ias.ac.in/currsci/oct102005/1200.pdf

Wallen, G. (1995, August 31). Summary of Events as recorded by USDA-APHIS Animal Care Inspector Wallen.

Wallen, G. (1995, September 7). Sworn Affidavit. VS form 3-59G. Government Exhibit 6-A

Website of African Lion Safari, Ontario, Canada http://www.lionsafari.com/home.html

Website of Busch Gardens, Tampa Bay. Retrieved from http://www.buschgardens.com/bg/

Website of waymarking.com. Information regarding Craig Road Pet Cemetery in Las Vegas, Nevada. Retrieved from http://www.waymarking.com/waymarks/WM632E_Craig_Road_Pet_Cemetery_Las_Vegas_NV

Weise, R.J., & Willis, K. (2004, August). Calculation of Longevity and Life Expectancy in Captive Elephants. *Zoo Biology, 23*(4). 365–373. Retrieved from http://onlinelibrary.wiley.com/doi/10. 1002/zoo.20011/abstract.

1. The famous and oft-debated picture of Mary hanging from the CC and O railroad derrick. Photo has entered public domain.
2. John Sparks (Charlie Sparks's father) and Mary in 1898. Photo has entered public domain.
3. Mike and Stoney, unknown location, taken by Sally LaTorres. Spring, 1985. One year before Mike and Sally's divorce. Stoney is almost twelve years old here. Stoney's transport trailer is seen to the left rear of him. Credit: Sally LaTorres
4. In the right background is the green and white travel trailer that served as LaTorres's quarters while working at the Luxor with Stoney. In the left background is the transport trailer Stoney traveled in his entire life. Stoney's barn, where he was kept during his injury, is just to the right (not pictured) of Mike's trailer. Credit: Linda Faso
5. Left background is LaTorres's quarters and to its immediate right is the open bay door of Stoney's barn behind the hotel. Credit Linda Faso
6. Linda Faso (right) and Loren Paglia (left) protesting outside the Luxor. Credit Linda Faso
7. Angela Faso (right) and Taloni Hart (left) protesting outside the Luxor. Credit Linda Faso
8. Protest outside Luxor on July 11, 1995. Credit Linda Faso
9. Protest outside Luxor. Credit Linda Faso
10. Protest outside Luxor. Credit Linda Faso
11. Assembled mourners at Stoney's funeral. Credit Linda Faso
12. Funeral offerings. Credit Linda Faso
13. Pat Derby of PAWS speaks at Stoney's funeral. Credit Linda Faso
14. Linda Faso speaks with supporters at funeral. Credit Linda Faso
15. Linda Faso addresses media at funeral with Stoney's grave behind her. Credit Linda Faso
16. Carroll Arnow in front of Stoney's grave. Credit Linda Faso
17. The blanket Carroll made for Stoney. One side reads "Mr. Magnificent," and the other "Stoney." Credit Linda Faso
18. Stoney's barn behind the Luxor being disassembled after his death. Credit Linda Faso
19. Another shot of the barn being disassembled with the slope of the Luxor in left background. Credit Linda Faso
20. Stoney's grave marker at Crag Road Pet Cemetary. Credit Linda Faso.

Elephants Among Us

15

16

17

18

19

20

EARTH

BOOKS

Earth Books are practical, scientific and philosophical publications about our relationship with the environment. Earth Books explore sustainable ways of living; including green parenting, gardening, cooking and natural building. They also look at ecology, conservation and aspects of environmental science, including green energy. An understanding of the interdependence of all living things is central to Earth Books, and therefore consideration of our relationship with other animals is important. Animal welfare is explored. The purpose of Earth Books is to deepen our understanding of the environment and our role within it. The books featured under this imprint will both present thought-provoking questions and offer practical solutions.